FINISHING OFF

FINISHING OFF

Patrick J. Galvin

Structures Publishing Co. 1977
Farmington, Michigan 48024

Manufactured in the United States of America

Edited by Shirley Horowitz

Designed by Patrick Mullaly

Cover design by Richard Kinney

Current Printing (last digit)
10   9   8   7   6   5   4   3   2   1

Library of Congress Cataloging in Publication Data

Galvin, Patrick J.
    Finishing off.

    Includes index.
    1. House construction — Amateurs' manuals. 2. Building-Details-Amateurs' manuals. I. Title.
TH4815.G36   643'.7   77.24521
ISBN O-912336-50-1
ISBN O-912336-51-X pbk.

Contents

1. Hands that rock the cradle can be
   worth thousands putting up wallboard   7

2. The first question is:
   Good grief! Why do all that myself?   9

3. Planning stage:
   The tools, the materials, the objectives   12

4. Partitions, doors, closets
   that can stay or move   16

5. Walls: The most visible spaces
   in your home's interior   20

6. Ceilings: Looking up can be great,
   no matter what your outlook is   46

7. Floors: How to cover them,
   from hardwood to resilient to carpeting   53

8. Basement use can double living space:
   or, how to upgrade life below grade   62

9. Attics: Space is limited, but
   you can do a lot with a little   89

10. Kitchens: Pick your best options   100

11. The Bathroom: Go in style   118

12. Garages: Conversions and room additions   130

    Manufacturers' Addresses   139

    Index   140

1. Hands that rock the cradle can be worth thousands putting up wallboard

You may own a home in which the basement or attic was never finished into living quarters . . . or a home that needs extensive remodeling . . . or you may want to convert your garage into usable living space.

Or perhaps you are buying a new home, and want to trim the cost by several thousand dollars; you are interested in what builders call "the affordable house," or the "basic" or "expandable" or "no-frills" house. Whatever they call it, it's a way for the new-home buyer to trim several thousand dollars off the purchase price.

He does this by permitting the builder to leave certain specified portions of the house unfinished. The buyer then provides many hours of his own labor, a few gallons of perspiration, various drops of blood and many well-chosen epithets. And he finishes the house himself.

It might include applying walls and wall coverings, finished flooring, ceilings, suspended and luminous ceilings, paneling, insulation, wiring, plumbing, painting, as well as creation of rooms in attics and basements. Some people even tackle the installation — after rough-in work has been completed — of bathroom and kitchen equipment.

The more it involves, the more the builder will chop off the selling price of the house, or the homeowner can save when remodeling.

But it's not all savings. The finishing materials must be purchased, along with the proper tools. The new finish-it-him(her)selfer must learn how to handle the tools and perform many operations, often at the risk of ruining some of the new-bought materials.

This means a lot of work. But it can also be a lot of fun.

The finish-it-yourselfers — let's call them F-I-Yers — have increased enormously in numbers in the last few years, for several reasons. The do-it-yourself trend, now at least 20 years old, which has involved both homeowners and apartment dwellers in repairs and small remodeling work, has contributed a lot of graduates to the F-I-Y trend. D-I-Y peeled away the many layers of mystique in plumbing, electrical work, tile-setting and other trades; homeowners en masse discovered studs, joists and subflooring.

This led to the great growth of the modern home center — which was once only a lumber yard — and with the home centers came instruction folders, clinics, new products adapted for amateur use, and books like this. Underlying it all were the tremendous increases in the costs of skilled labor and in the services of the specialized contractors. Skilled labor rates of $25 an hour are not unusual today, and with the increased costs of doing business, a contractor often must charge a customer twice that.

At the same time land prices have soared, as have taxes and the prices of new homes. So a few years ago builders started promoting what they called "the no-frills home" in an effort to make homes more affordable.

The public response was not very positive. We didn't want them to impose smaller rooms, fewer baths on us. We and they compromised, and settled for options. We might opt to have the builder leave out the second bath and the powder room, but we would have him rough them in so we could add them later. We might ask him to leave the third and fourth bedrooms unfinished, with bare studs, so we could finish them later. Most of all, we would opt for him to leave attics and basements bare, and later we would create entire rooms ourselves.

So, to pick one recent year (1976) builders built 1,225,000 single-family homes. Many had no attics or the space there was unusable; 67,500 usable attics were left unfinished. And of 588,000 that had full or partial basements, 529,000 were left unfinished. (These estimates are by the Bureau of Building Marketing Research, based on Department of Commerce data.)

Don't be misled on savings. As a F-I-Yer, you will pay retail prices for all the materials you buy, and these prices are much higher than what your builder would pay.

On the other hand, putting all those materials plus the builder's services and labor on your 30-year mortgage, would just about double their price because you would be paying interest on them all those years.

As an F-I-Yer you will make the choice of when to finish off, hence when to pay it. If you won't need the extra one or two bedrooms for two years, presumably you will be making more money then and will be better able to afford the materials you will need and possibly even the addition of some skilled help.

So think it over first. Consult with your builder on the possible savings and evaluate your own capabilities.

This 10 x 16 room is typical of unfinished spaces in many of today's new homes, and is far more finished than many. (Top left) The homeowner first installed vertical planks to wall, then (top right) horizontal planks, and made the simple shutters. The family then added hollow-core doors to create an accent wall (center left), and Chandelier acoustical ceiling tile. Self-stick floor tiles came next (center right) as other members of the family got into the act. With new tools and new expertise, they started to create their own furniture (bottom left), and ended up with a finished room on which they saved $1,500. Best of all, they got a lot of help from manufacturers. For a step-by-step booklet on how to create this room, write to Armstrong Cork for their "I-Did-It-Myself" book (See manufacturer index).

2. The first question is: Good grief! Why do all that myself?

Make no mistake. It will be work. Lots of work. And it will be your own home, so you won't want poor workmanship. It must be done right!

So why should you try?

Because it's the only way you can afford the kind of home you want. That's why.

Thinking Positive

You have to sell yourself on that if you are going to do the work yourself. But thousands, many thousands, are doing it each year as land and building costs soar, as rentals skyrocket, and as, year after year, your own home turns out to be one of the best possible investments.

You already are at least partially sold on this premise, or you wouldn't be reading this book. But to finish the sales job, let's break the question down, point by point.

Land and Housing Costs

We don't have to belabor this, you've already looked into it. But the prices of some lots I have looked at have gone up 1500 percent in the last dozen years. The house you would have paid $30,000 to build two years ago will now cost $42,000 to build.

We know land will continue to go up, because it is getting scarcer in the places most of us want to live. And to this growing scarcity we must add an annual inflation factor, plus the increasing problems of local and regional environmental restrictions that take land out of the housing market.

In other words, there is pressure on us to decide and act now.

Tax Benefits

The tax advantages of home ownership cannot be overemphasized. When you live in an apartment, you are paying the landlord's taxes in your rental payments. When you own your own home you pay your own taxes, and all taxes are deductible from your income taxes. Further, interest payments are deductible, and most of your mortgage payments for the first several years are interest.

So if you pay $300 per month in rent, the money is gone. But if you pay $300 a month on a mortgage, around $200 of it could be deductible, depending on the amount of your down payment.

Taxes will continue to grow, and there seems to be no way to avoid it. If you gain a rebate here and there from the federal government, it is eaten up by local school taxes. In rental, you can only pay and complain. With home ownership, you may pay and complain, but you'll always get some of it back.

You Can Do It Your Way

In an apartment you can change the wallpaper and the floor covering and buy new furniture. But you will eventually be held accountable if you put holes in the walls or in any way damage the landlord's property.

But in your own home, it *is* your home. If you want a pass-through cut in the wall from kitchen to dining room or to the rec room, you can do it. You can add a bathroom or a powder room, construct a storage wall — it's all yours. And this is a wonderful freedom. It comes only with home ownership, adding to the pressure on us to do it now.

Four More Reasons To Do It Yourself

There are some more good reasons for finishing it yourself, despite the fact that it might involve unknown skills and countless hours of labor.

First, you get more house. The $5,000 you save (to pick a figure) may mean that you can buy a 3-bedroom house instead of one with only two bedrooms, or one with two and a half bathrooms instead of only one. You spend the same money, but you end up with a lot more. And you'll get a lot more when you sell the house.

If you need a 3-bedroom, 2-bathroom house, and right now you have only enough savings to swing the down payment for a 2-bedroom, 1-bathroom builder-finished house — let's say the difference is $6,000 — and if your mortgage lender wants the customary down payment of 20 percent to 30 percent, it means you must wait until you have another $1,200 to $2,000 for the down payment. How long will that take? A year, perhaps? By then you may need another $600 to put down, at the rate housing is going up, and your house can easily cost 20 percent more. Finishing it yourself lets you buy now, before prices go up again (and there's absolutely no reason to think they might stop going up).

Second, your "sweat equity" makes your house worth more immediately. For example, if you will pay $30,000 for your unfinished home, it would be worth, say, $36,000 if it were fully finished at the moment you buy it. If you complete the finishing-off a year later, it would then be worth the normal increase in value, perhaps 20 percent *plus* the $6,000 in free labor you put into it. Your investment has increased by the amount of work you put into it.

Third, it is a worthwhile family activity. The whole family gets into the act with their own allotted jobs. All learn a lot, acquire skills, and the kids will have a lot more respect for the house at play time.

And fourth, it'll keep you off the streets.

But — *Can* I Finish It Myself?

In a word, yes. You wouldn't believe the vast amount of help available to you. You wouldn't believe, you who think you are "all thumbs," how much you can do and how well you can do it by *slowing down* and *thinking it through*.

First, check with your builder. Many builders not only offer you options on what they will leave unfinished, but a few even provide all interior materials.

As an example of how far a builder can go to be helpful, Ridge Homes (division of Evans Products) combines such products as Evans lumber, Alcoa siding, General Electric, Progress Lighting, American Standard, Armstrong, Wenczel tile and I-T-E. When you buy one of their unfinished homes, the Ridge builder includes all interior materials *cut to fit*, plus manuals detailing how to do it. There are separate manuals on plumbing, electrical work, installing the heating plant — the whole works. And there are other companies who will do the same.

Along with the many manufacturers offering free literature that tells how to do practically any operation, there are books. The "Successful" series, of which this is one, includes books on everything from painting to actually building your own home.

Then there are the friends, relatives, neighbors. Many will delight in helping. Many will trade off if you suggest it. For example, if you are a plumber yourself, or a skilled amateur at this or any other trade, find a neighbor or friend who has some other skill. He will need you for something, just as you need him for something.

If there are some things you are really afraid to try, and if you cannot find a skilled friend or neighbor who will

help, contract them out. Ask your builder for three dependable firms in that trade, write a description of the job to be done and send a copy of the description, with a copy of your blueprint, to each of the three and ask for a bid. But do not accept the lowest bid without first discussing quality of product and workmanship with the bidder. Remember, you want an inexpensive job, not a cheap job.

Codes and Permits

There are some areas where local law requires that the work be done by a pro. This pertains particularly to electrical work and plumbing. Other areas require only an inspection by a local building inspector while the work is in progress and after it is finished. You will pay a fee for this. Incidentally, even the pro's work is subject to these inspections. In a rural area you are more likely to be free to do everything yourself, but check with the county and township first. They might fine you for bypassing them.

Obstacles

There are potential problems, and you should be aware of them. Some mortgage lenders will not have any faith in your abilities. They figure an unfinished house is only an unfinished house. They might refuse to give you a mortgage entirely, or try to cut it down by requiring more down payment.

In addition, some builders are not interested in working this way. Either they will not sell unfinished, or they will not mark down enough to make it interesting to you.

Do not blame them; it's their business, and they have a right to run it the way they think best. A builder often feels he is providing you the best service by doing it all professionally.

The point is, do not give up if you cannot find what you want on the first try. Check your real estate ads and your phone book and other ads for builders who will do it your way. Often you will find these builders already have cleared the way with the mortgage lenders. If you have a favorite builder and want to deal with him, go see him and talk it over. He may have been dead set against F-I-Yers last month. But this month he may need the business.

Just be very sure of what you are getting on the deal. Be prepared to inspect a written agreement which tells exactly what the builder will do and what he will not do. Builders who specialize in unfinished homes will have all of this information in printed form. Other builders might not have it, and you must protect yourself.

EXTERIOR

FRAMING

Floor Joists — 2 x 8 or 2 x 10 (per plan) on 16″ centers with steel bridging, ready to install for extra rigidity. 2 x 6 foundation sill plates, and 6 x 10. built-up main beam.

Wall Framing—2 x 4 on 16″ centers. All corners two 2 x 4 corner studs. All window openings supported by a 4 x 10 or two 2 x 10 solid headers.

Wall Sheathing — ½″ thick 4 x 8 plywood on all corners, ½″ asphalt impregnated insulating wall sheathing for increased structural rigidity and weather resistance.

Ceiling Joists — 2 x 6 on 16″ centers pre-cut, and beveled. 2 x 4 stay board supplied for leveling, spacing, and stiffening each span of ceiling joists.

Roof Rafters — 2 x 6 on 16″ centers pre-cut and notched, supported by a 2 x 8 ridge board and tied together by 1 x 6 collar beams.

Gable Walls — 2 x 4 on 16″ centers with ½″ asphalt impregnated insulating wall sheathing, 2 x 6 plate.

ROOFING

Sheathing — ⅜″ thick 4 x 8 plywood for firm construction.

Shingles — Asphalt shingles over 15 lb. asphalt saturated felt. Self-seal for extra weather protection with 15 years guarantee. Roof edges are protected and supported by aluminum roof edging around entire perimeter.

Gutter and Downspout — 5″ K-type galvanized gutter with 2 x 3″ downspout. Slip joint connectors, end caps, spikes and ferrules, elbows, and shoes, are included.

Flashing — Aluminum flashing included for all valleys and chimneys.

WALL FINISH

Siding — Factory primed horizontal manufactured siding at 11″ exposure, with primed metal corners and primed manufactured vertical siding for front where specified.

Trim — Factory primed ⅜″ thick exterior plywood for soffit, 1 x 6 fascia, and 1 x 6 barge boards, aluminum soffit vents and gable louvers are included to eliminate attic condensation.

MILLWORK

Doors — 1¾″ thick primed Steel insulated front and rear doors, both pre-hung with hardware, weather stripping, and aluminum threshold installed. Drip cap where specified.

Windows — Primed white pine double-hung factory assembled with balances and weather stripping, ready to be set into the wall. Window and door blinds are included where specified. Caulking is supplied.

INTERIOR

WALLS

Framing — All partitions, bearing and non-bearing, are pre-cut 2 x 4 on 16″ centers for 8 feet ceiling height with double top plates. Semi-assembled door bucks with 4 x 10 or two 2 x 10 headers.

Insulation — 3½″ thick fiberglass with R-11 rating for exterior walls and entire ceiling area. Staples for insulation included.

Wall Covering — Choice of ½″ gypsum drywall board in 4 x 8 and 4 x 12 sheets complete with spackling cement, joint tape, and metal corner beads. In the bathrooms, your choice of colors in ceramic wall tile in the tub or shower alcove, 6 feet high from the floor.

DOORS

Passage doors are semi-assembled pre-hung mahogany flush with hinges installed, drilled for lockset. Each closet has mahogany flush wood sliding doors.

MILLWORK

Trim — Solid clear grade white pine casing, jamb, door stops, sash bead, stool, apron, baseboard, and floor molding. Pin rails and shelving for all closets included.

INTERIOR (Continued)

Stairways — Basement stairway includes handrail, post, pre-cut stringers, and treads. Where specified, finished stairway is pre-assembled, pre-fit, and pre-drilled. It includes fir or yellow pine treads and risers, white pine newel, handrail, and balusters, and all other accessories applicable.

FLOORING

Subfloor — ½″ thick 4 x 8 plywood for a strong floor platform.

Finished Floor — 100% continuous filament nylon carpet over 60 oz. waffle foam rubber padding, installed over ⅝″ underlayment or 25/32″ x 2¼″ #1 oak hardwood flooring, tongue and grooved and end matched, installed over red rosin building paper. A clear super-gloss one step protective coating is also included. Vinyl-asbestoes floor tile for bath and kitchen areas.

HARDWARE

Nails — An adequate supply of nails of all sizes and types required in accordance with standard building procedures.

Finished Hardware — Brass finish doorlocks, hinges, sash locks, handrail brackets and aluminum closet rods.

PLUMBING

Rough — A custom designed "PVC" or "ABS" plastic drainage system complete with all fittings, and ½″ M copper tubing water lines with fittings.

Finish — Fixtures include wall hung lavatory plus water closet in white, and with the Good Housekeeping seal of approval. Also, a matching seat and cover. Family bathroom includes tub; master bathroom features stall shower with tempered safety glass enclosure, plus water closet and wall hung lavatory. Powder room includes water closet and wall hung vitreous china lavatory.

Bathroom Accessories — Mirror/medicine cabinet and bar light fixture. Also chrome towel bar, toothbrush and tumbler holder, soap and grab bar, paper holder and shower curtain rod.

HEATING

Furnace — Oil fired, forced warm air, with automatic controls and safety switch and 275 gal. oil tank and fittings. Pre-fab chimney where specified.

Ductwork — Customized square trunk supply system with round runoffs to each individual room, including all dampers and registers, and a square trunk and panned joist return system including return grilles.

Hot Water — Glass lined gas or electric, quick recovery domestic hot water heater complete with safety relief valve.

ELECTRIC

Rough — 100 Amp service with switch type circuit breaker panel. All necessary ceiling and wall boxes as per the latest requirements of the National Underwriters' Laboratory Code.

Wire — Wire package includes sufficient amount of 12/2 and 14/2 copper wire and breakers to complete all house circuits per Ridge Homes Utility Plan; also, proper amount of correct size of both wire and breakers are supplied to install all appliances and utlities purchased from Ridge Homes.

Finish — Your choice of Traditional, Contemporary, or Modern style lighting fixtures individually designed for your home. All necessary receptacles, switches, plates, and accessories are included. Bedrooms have switched receptacle.

KITCHEN

Cabinets — Each kitchen layout has been designed to give the maximum amount of cabinet space and work area. Your choice of Contemporary or Aquarius cabinets. All wall cabinets feature adjustable shelves.

Sink and Counter Top — The single bowl steel sink in your choice of colors complete with all fittings, faucet. The counter top is post-formed Formica in your choice of pattern and color. Wall mounted exhaust fan included.

---

*Illustrations and floor plan dimensions of all houses are approximate. Materials and labor for landscaping, sidewalks, driveways, paint, masonry, septic tanks, garages, stone, brick and special sidings illustrated or referred to are not included in the basic prices of the homes.

**Materials listed above that are not included in the standard plans for expandable areas are available at additional cost.

When you buy an unfinished home, be sure you get all specifications in writing. This sheet from Ridge Homes is representative of the kind of information you should get. You should get another form detailing precisely what the builder will finish and what you will be responsible for.

3. Planning stage: The tools, the materials, the objectives

First Steps

The first important step is to deposit some knowledge in that bank between your ears. Home centers everywhere are conducting clinics for all kinds of in-home construction and finishing activities. Watch for them. Go to them. Pick up the free literature you will find there. If you go to three or four of these clinics you can end up with free literature that will aid you in nearly every finishing operation in your home.

Use this time to check out tool and equipment rental. There are certain tools you know you'll want to buy, because you can use them over and over for years. These include basic hand tools — hammers, screw drivers, wood chisels, crow bars, saws, basic power tools such as a radial, and a jig saw and a drill, a 4-foot level and a shorter one.

But there are other tools you will want to rent, such as a flooring nailer to install your hardwood flooring, or a carpet-kicker to install your wall-to-wall carpet. It would be a waste to buy these items since you will use them only one time, and never again.

Tool rental rates vary widely; there are no norms. In checking this, I found that a single rental firm in a small town might charge rates twice as high as in a nearby city where there is competition. So use this time to locate a rental tool agency you can live with, one that has the assortment you'll need at a reasonable price.

Survey the home supply stores for materials. There will be new materials on the market that you might know nothing about. This includes such things as cultured marble for bathroom sinks or countertops or for walls, tubs and showers made of reinforced glass fiber, polyurethane and polystyrene imitation wood beams for your ceilings, artificial brick and stone for your walls, or genuine brick and stone veneers — there are new things coming out every day and you should know about them before you start.

Think about your color schemes. It sometimes takes days to settle on paint colors, carpet colors, paneling colors and patterns, and you should have a general decorating motif for every room of your home before you are faced with the need to buy the paint and the panels.

Apportion your expenditures. You will want to finish off your basic living quarters first, as soon as possible. It will take money, quite a lot of it if this will include bathroom and kitchen. So if you won't get around to paneling the basement for four months (be realistic) you should not tie up your cash in materials for the basement. Get around and get prices on the materials you will need first, as well as the tools, so you can buy without budget strain.

Insulation

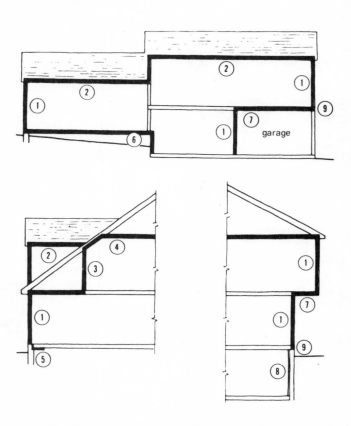

Specific areas that require insulation are: (1) exterior walls and walls between unheated and heated parts of the house; (2) ceilings with cold spaces above, and dormer ceilings; (3) knee walls when attic is finished; (4) between collar beams and rafters; (5) around perimeter of slab; (6) floors above vented crawl spaces; (7) floors above unheated or open spaces, garage or porch; (8) basement walls when space is finished off; (9) in back of band or header joists. (Mineral Wool Insulation Assn., Inc.)

Think energy savings all the way, and plan insulation where you can. Almost every public utility has literature on saving energy. Get it. You can write the U. S. Department of Commerce at the National Bureau of Standards (Washington DC 20234) for its booklet "Making the Most of Your Energy Dollars" and ask for other consumer information on energy.* You may find, for example, that proper and adequate insulation might pay back its cost in energy savings in as little as a few months, or as long as 39 years, depending on your fuel and location. To determine your needs, see the accompanying map and chart.

* For comprehensive information on how to save energy and money in your home, see *How to Cut Your Energy Bills*, a *Successful* Book by Ronald Derven and Carol Nichols.

SUMMER COOLING ZONES

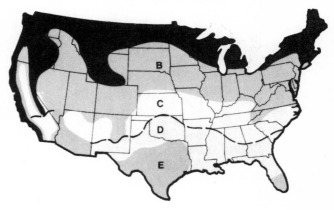

MATERIAL REQUIRED TO ACHIEVE R-19

The minimum insulative value for best energy savings is R-11; the requirement escalates in colder areas. As shown above, a 6-inch layer of fiberglass insulation has the same insulation (R-19, for colder climates) as more than 14 feet of sand or gravel (CertainTeed Products).

ATTIC INSULATION FOR SUMMER COOLING						
AIR CONDITIONING COST		RECOMMENDED INSULATION				
ELECTRIC (kWh)	GAS (therm)	ZONE A	ZONE B	ZONE C	ZONE D	ZONE E
1.5¢	9¢	—	—	—	R-11	R-11
2¢	12¢	—	—	R-11	R-11	R-11
2.5¢	15¢	—	—	R-11	R-11	R-19
3¢	18¢	—	R-11	R-11	R-11	R-19
4¢	24¢	—	R-11	R-11	R-19	R-30
5¢	30¢	—	R-11	R-19	R-19	R-30
6¢	36¢	—	R-11	R-19	R-30	R-30

WINTER HEATING ZONES

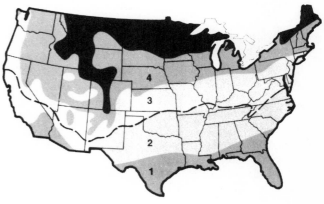

Finished or unfinished attics require insulation, although in different parts of the space. (Dept. of Housing & Urban Development)

ATTIC INSULATION FOR WINTER HEATING								
HEATING COST				RECOMMENDED INSULATION				
GAS (therm)	OIL (gallon)	ELECTRIC RESISTANCE (kWh)	ELECTRIC HEAT PUMP (kWh)	ZONE 1	ZONE 2	ZONE 3	ZONE 4	ZONE 5
9¢	13¢	—	1¢	—	R-11	R-11	R-19	R-19
12¢	17¢	—	1.3¢	—	R-11	R-19	R-19	R-30
15¢	21¢	—	1.7¢	—	R-11	R-19	R-30	R-30
18¢	25¢	1¢	2¢	—	R-11	R-19	R-30	R-30
24¢	34¢	1.3¢	2.6¢	R-11	R-19	R-30	R-33	R-38
30¢	42¢	1.6¢	3.3¢	R-11	R-19	R-30	R-33	R-38
36¢	50¢	2¢	4¢	R-11	R-30	R-33	R-38	R-44
54¢	75¢	3¢	6¢	R-11	R-30	R-38	R-49	R-49
72¢	$1.00	4¢	8¢	R-19	R-38	R-44	R-49	R-60
90¢	$1.25	5¢	10¢	R-19	R-38	R-49	R-57	R-66

Find the amount of insulation you need on these weather maps and tables. (CertainTeed)

TYPE OF INSULATION

	BATTS OR BLANKETS		LOOSE FILL (POURED-IN)			
	glass fiber	rock wool	glass fiber	rock wool	cellulosic fiber	
R-11	3½"-4"	3"	5"	4"	3"	R-11
R-19	6"-6½"	5¼"	8"-9"	6"-7"	5"	R-19
R-22	6½"	6"	10"	7"-8"	6"	R-22
R-30	9½"-10½"*	9"*	13"-14"	10"-11"	8"	R-30
R-38	12"-13"*	10½"*	17"-18"	13"-14"	10"-11"	R-38

* two batts or blankets required.

This table gives R-values for different thicknesses of insulation. (Dept. of Housing & Urban Development)

What You Should Know About Nails and Screws

Nails and screws will fill a big part of your life for the next several months. Here are some basics about them.

Nails

Nail sizes are graduated in quarter-inches from 1 to 6 inches. The sizes are designated in "pennies", for which the symbol is d. A 2d nail is 1 inch long. A 6d nail is 2 inches long. A 10d nail is 3 inches long. The numbers between represent quarter-inch changes in length. But the size after 10d is 12d, which is 3-1/4 inches long, and the next size is 16d, 3-1/2 inches long. A 4-inch nail is 20d, a 5-inch nail is 40d, and a 6-inch nail is 60d.

Common nails have a large head and are used for most general work.

Finishing nails have practically no head and are used where the nailheads should not show; they are sunk into the wood with a punch.

Casing nails are similar, but are stronger.

Spiral nails look somewhat like screws, and are used for flooring, as they won't pull loose to permit squeaks. A variation is the *ring* nail, with annular rings that also increase holding power.

Brads are used for paneling; they are like finishing nails but have less strength.

Duplex head nails are used for temporary installations. They are like common nails, but have two heads so one can be driven tight and the other protrude for pulling out.

Concrete nails, or *case-hardened* nails, are used for nailing furring strips to concrete walls, or wall baseplates to concrete floors.

In nailing wood to wood, you usually nail the thinner piece to the thicker piece, and the nail should have 2/3 of its length in the thicker piece, for holding power. This does not apply to concrete nails, which should not go more than 1 inch into concrete or 1-1/4 inch into masonry block.

When using concrete nails, always wear goggles, since the nails tend to shatter rather than bend.

When you nail near the edge of a board, blunt the end of the nail to prevent splitting. A sharp nail point wedges through the wood, leading to splits, while a blunt point tears the wood fiber so there is less chance of splits.

Screws

Screws will not see as much use as nails, but there may be places where you will want their extra holding power. Or there might be places in your basement paneling where you will want occasional access to pipes or wiring, and at such locations you might want to use screws.

Screws will have slots or cross-slots for the screwdriver; cross-slots take the screwdriver known as a Phillips head.

Try to settle on one type, or you will usually find you have the wrong screwdriver in your hand.

Screws have round heads, oval heads or flat heads. The flat heads are most common because they countersink themselves flush with the wood surface or slightly below. Oval heads countersink and leave a round head protruding.

There also are metal screws called self-tapping, or thread-cutting, identifiable because the thread comes all the way to the head. You might want to use these if you are connecting ductwork. You will have to drill a pilot hole first, slightly smaller than the screw.

A Quick Guide to Adhesives

There are many different kinds of adhesives on the market, most of which you will never use. There are a thousand brand names, and it is often hard to tell from the name what type of adhesive it is. Always read labels carefully to see what the adhesive is engineered to do, and how easy it is to use.

Mastic adhesives are used for bonding wall paneling to furring strips or wallboard. They also can be used for wall, ceiling and floor tiles.

PVA adhesives are the common "white glues" that have all kinds of uses, and often are used in woodworking and repairs in the house.

Contact adhesives are used for bonding plastic laminates to your countertop substrate, or any other place you might use plastic laminates. The water-based contacts are harder to use, but solvent-based contacts are highly flammable. You can't "work" with these. You coat both surfaces, wait until they are dry to the touch, then join the pieces, and once joined you can't budge either piece. You must get it right the first time. Contacts are good for other joining jobs, such as plastic to steel, or wood to wood.

Rubber cements are good for bonding many materials, but they have no structural strength.

Silicone sealants have adhesive qualities, but are more often used for sealing adjoining surfaces of your tub or sink, or for Corian seams.

Epoxy adhesives will glue just about anything to anything but they are cumbersome to use. You have to mix two components, one to one, and this works best for small jobs.

4. Partitions, doors, closets that can stay or move

As you gain skills and confidence, new ideas will come to you. You will realize, possibly, that you'll need a closet here or there that wasn't provided in the original floorplan. Or you will want to create closets and other walls in the unfinished basement and attic.

In some places these might be permanent. But there's an old custom in northern Italy that is worth considering. There, nearly all interior walls are only semi-permanent. They put in walls to create rooms during the young, growing times of a family. And as the youngsters grow and move away, the walls can be removed. This means that as the family dwindles the master bedroom, for example, can be expanded into a more luxurious suite that could not be afforded earlier, or two small bedrooms can be combined into a pool room. Normally, storage walls are made up of floor-to-ceiling cabinets that include closet areas.

We will show you some pictures of such ideas in this chapter. But first, let's look at some simple steps for building walls, closets and bathrooms.

Partitions

To put up a partition that you can some day remove, use 2x3 and 1x3 lumber. Use the 1x3s for base plate and top plate, and cut them to the length of your partition. You will then use the 2x3s as studs, placed 16 inches apart, center to center.

Make this partition flat on the floor, to be tilted up into position when the framing is completed. This means you will have to make the partition 1/2-inch shorter than the floor-to-ceiling height to allow room to tilt it up, and then you will have to shim it up tight with plenty of shims on both sides along the floor to make it solid.

Nailing

Mark off the base and top plates together for the studs, so you will be sure they are vertical, 16 inches apart on center. You can then put one nail into each stud through first one plate, then the other, and tilt the partition up into position. Then toe-nail the studs to the base plate, driving

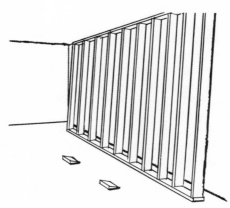

Wedges can be used to tighten the frame to the ceiling.

the nails at an angle of about 45 degrees to fasten the stud securely. Do the same at the top plate.

Now check to see if your partition is going across the floor joists, or in the same direction. You will want to nail the base plate securely to the floor, and this means into the joists. If you are going across joists, fine. Nail into the joists. But if you are going in the same direction, you will have to go underneath and install a bridging of 2x4s between the joists, flanking the line of your partition, so it can be nailed solidly.

This applies equally to the ceiling. If you are creating an upstairs closet with this partition, you will have to go into the attic and provide the bridging.

In nailing in your new partition, you might consider using duplex head nails, because this is a partition you may some day want to take out. A duplex head nail has two heads. One can be driven tight, and the other sticks up far enough so you can remove it.

What size nails? It's a good rule-of-thumb, in all of your work, that 2/3 of the length of the nail should be in the piece you are nailing *to.* In nailing 1x3s to the floor, the actual size of a 1x3 is 3/4 inch thick and 2-1/2 inches wide. You will want nails 2-1/4 inches long for your partition, which is a 7d size. And you want "common" nails. Don't use "finishing" nails which have very small heads and pull through the wood easily.

Paneling and Wiring

With your partition up in place, you can cover it with wallboard or paneling. But first consider whether you will want wall outlets in it. If so, drill holes through the studs to bring the wire in from the wall. If you decide you won't want wiring, remember you will quite probably change your mind later; now, while the wall is open, bring the wiring in and cap it. Or better yet, go ahead and put a double outlet on either side.

Closets and Bathrooms

Now let's consider a permanent closet, or a bath or powder room.

For this you will want 2x4s all around, for studs and for base and top plates. You also will have to frame a door.

First, remember that doors come in different sizes. So first buy the door, then you will be sure to make the opening the right size. The opening will have to be large enough to allow for framing and for 1/4 inch clearance at the bottom and 1/8 inch on each side. If the door will open over a carpet, bottom clearance must be 7/8 inch. If it will be a bathroom door, you will want an extra 1/2 inch of space at the bottom to permit air to be drawn in when the ventilating fan is on; otherwise the fan won't do a decent job of venting.

It is also possible to buy door frames that are already built. They come in assemblies consisting of header, pocket framework, face jamb, and hanging hardware. The door itself is purchased separately, in the desired style and width. If you choose this route, buy the frame before leaving room for the opening, so the opening will be the right size.

You will be using 8d common nails for this job. Follow the same procedure as you did for the temporary partition, but use 2x4s for base and top plates as well as for studs. Put the base and top plates together on the floor to put down marks for studs, 16 inches on center, after cutting them to

Door and Window Openings

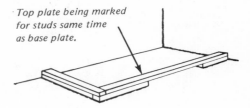

Fig. 1—Base Plate and Top Plate

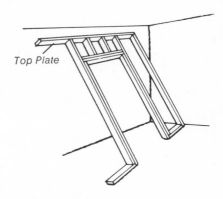

Fig. 2—Wall Section

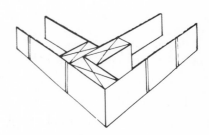

Fig. 3—Inside and Outside Corner Nailing Surfaces

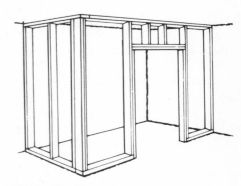

Fig. 4—Structure

1: When nailing the base plate to the floor, leave an opening for the door frame. Measure and mark the top and base plates for placement of the studs, which should be toe-nailed 16 inches on center. Wood cut from base plate to form opening becomes header for doorway opening.

2: Tilt up wall frame and nail to floor and ceiling.

3: The outside corner is made up from three 2x4's and installed so that it provides inside and outside nailing surfaces that are as thick as the other studs. Now add drywall to inside of closet.

4: Plywood paneling may be nailed directly to the studs. Once the panels are up, install the door frame. Then add corner molding, cove molding, and base molding.

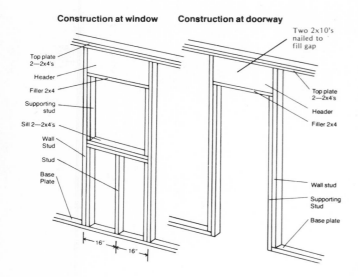

Construction at window **Construction at doorway**

Top plate 2—2x4's
Header
Filler 2x4
Supporting stud
Sill 2—2x4's
Wall Stud
Stud
Base Plate

Two 2x10's nailed to fill gap
Top plate 2—2x4's
Header
Filler 2x4
Wall stud
Supporting Stud
Base plate

16"   16"

length. Your top plate will be one piece. You will have cut a gap in the base plate for the door, and the piece you cut out will move to the top of the doorway to become the "header." Cut another piece the same length to make a double header.

In your finishing-off process, you might find that you want to cut an additional doorway in an existing wall. This is a bit different, in that the double-header at the top must support the weight of the structure above.

In this case, your double-header should consist of two 2x10s or two 2x12s nailed together so they fill the gap between your door framing and the joist above. You'll then add a 2x4 under the double-header, laid flat to match the thickness of the studs, so you will have an even surface for applying wallboard. The drawing shows this kind of double-header with the 2x4 filler below.

Rooms that Change Size as Your Family Changes

Earlier we mentioned the Italian custom of making walls semi-permanent. This is one of the great luxuries you can consider when you buy your house unfinished. Your builder will have to put in certain walls that are load-bearing, that support the weight of the house. But perhaps you can discuss this with him so you end up with a minimum of walls upstairs, to give you more flexibility.

This plan sets up walls that are, in themselves, closets of a sort. Shelves are combined with drawers and wardrobes and cabinets. There are various prebuilt systems made for this, some foreign and some domestic. Or you can make your own systems using standard kitchen wall cabinets.

Two companies that offer these systems in the U.S. are Living Wall and Interwall. There are also imported lines, but they are usually more expensive, and more difficult to locate. Living Wall's cabinet systems are 78 inches high (18

inches shorter than standard wall height) and 16-1/2 or 17-1/2 inches deep. But you could easily build a floor-to-ceiling wall of plywood or particleboard to attach to the back of the system, and finish it off with molding at the ceiling.

Kitchen cabinets are available everywhere and can be combined easily to make wall systems. You can find them with fine furniture finishes, or with plastic laminate finishes such as Formica in dozens of different woodgrain finishes or bright colors.

We suggested kitchen wall cabinets for this because they are only 15 inches deep, whereas base cabinets are 24 inches deep. You might not be able to afford to give up 24 inches of space for a wall, but you can give up 15 inches when you consider that they also are storage walls and eliminate the need for closets. You might have to go to a kitchen specialist to get the choice of cabinets you want, because other kinds of cabinet outlets seldom have the variety.

Standard heights of kitchen wall cabinets are 30 inches. Another standard height is 18 inches. The standard height for your rooms will be 96 inches. So the combination of two of each cabinet size would make your wall floor to ceiling, in the simplest form. But you also could combine 18-inch and 15-inch cabinets for a pattern of open shelves and closed cabinets.

Look at the pictures, and make your choice.

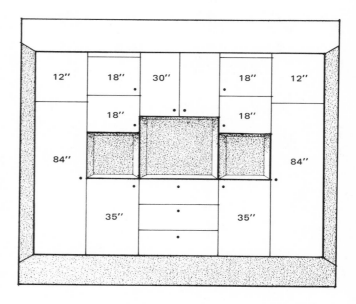

12"	18"	30"		18"	12"
84"	18"			18"	84"
	35"			35"	

Kitchen Cabinet Units combine here to create a wall. At both ends are tall 84 in. cabinets for wardrobes. These are 24 in. deep. Two base units next to them also are 24 in. deep. All other units are 15 in. deep, set flush on this side, making decorative table spaces on other side in other room. Three areas in center have been left open for shelves or decorative items, but backed with plywood for a full-privacy barrier between rooms.

These Living Walls combinations are only 78 in. high, and would have to be built up at the top with plywood to make a complete wall. But they show the combinations possible to provide storage, and they can be moved to change rooms as family grows.

Floor-to-Ceiling units by Interwall need no buildup. They also have wardrobe units for full closet function. When these are used as wall no partition is needed behind them.

5. Walls: The most visible spaces in your home's interior

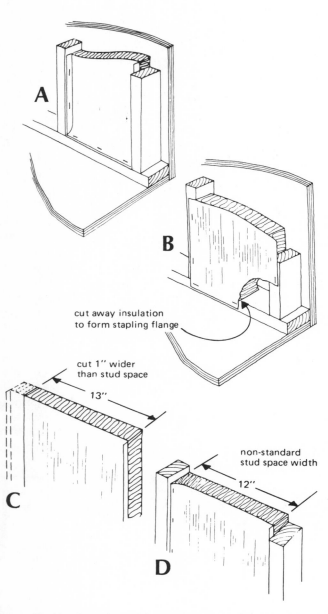

A

B

cut away insulation
to form stapling flange

cut 1" wider
than stud space

13"

C

non-standard
stud space width

12"

D

Working from the top down, space staples 8 in. apart, fitting flanges tightly against sides (A) or faces (B) or studs. Insulate nonstandard width spaces by cutting the insulation and vapor barrier an inch or so wider than the space to be filled (C). Staple uncut flange as usual. Pull the vapor barrier on the cut side to the other stud, compressing the insulation behind it, and staple through vapor barrier (D). (National Mineral Wood Insulation Assn., Inc.)

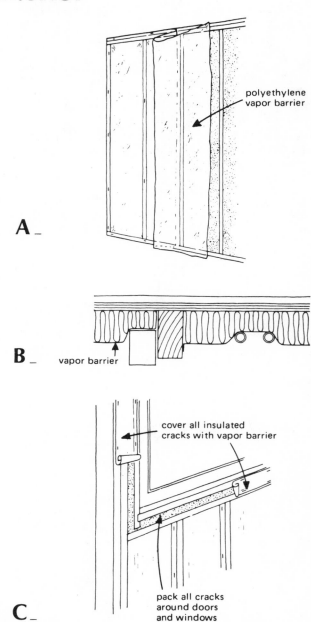

A

polyethylene
vapor barrier

B

vapor barrier

C

cover all insulated
cracks with vapor barrier

pack all cracks
around doors
and windows

Wedge pressure-fit blankets into space to get a highly effective vapor barrier. Cover the inside face of the wall studs with polyethylene sheet (A). (B) Push insulation behind pipes, ducts and electrical boxes. (C) Pack small spaces between rough framing and door and window headers, jambs, and sills with pieces of insulation. Staple over with vapor barrier. (National Mineral Wool Insulation Assn., Inc.)

The walls of your new home will probably end up as a pretty mixed bag in their finished state. You'll have a combination of painted gypsum board in some rooms, wood paneling in others, perhaps some ceramic tile in the bathroom, or exotic touches such as mirrored walls here and there. Many homeowners like to use vinyl or other patterned wallcovering for decorative effect.

You probably are starting with totally unfinished walls in attic and basement, and sheetrocked walls in the regular living area.

In some cases, however, you will be looking at bare studs throughout the house. If so, look first at the wiring and plumbing rough-in and check them for completeness. The builder might have roughed in, or you might have had it subcontracted. Or perhaps you did it yourself. But think now, before the final finishing, about what you might want a few years from now. Add now the rough-in for conveniences you cannot afford now but may want in the future, such as an extra bathroom or half-bath, plumbing for a bar, or gas or electricity for a barbecue grill you may want to add later. Rough-in materials are cheap, and it is easier to do it now.*

Insulation

With rough-in completed, and if your studs are still bare, install insulation on all outside walls if it has not already been installed. Use the blanket type, Fiberglas in heavy paper. The paper acts as a vapor shield to prevent condensation that could later rot your framework. Use a staple gun to fasten insulation blankets about 3/4-inch from the front edge of the framing. This will give you a pocket of air behind the blanket that will aid the work of the insulation.

If you are going to finish off part of the attic, be sure you surround the living area there with insulation. This means installing insulation in the rafters and the walls; blankets or batts can be put between roof rafters or end walls. Fit one end of the blanket or batt snugly against the top piece of the framing (as in illustration) with the vapor barrier facing into the heated attic space. Also tuck insulation in around all of the rough-in and leave no gaps. It will lower your heating and cooling bills in all the years ahead.

How to Install Wallboard

Gypsum wallboard, the most commonly used material for walls in today's homes, comes in 4x8- and 4x12-foot sheets. It is made of gypsum bonded between two sheets of tough protective paper, and all of the edges are tapered to allow for filling and taping the joints to achieve a smooth surface. If the outside temperature is below 55 degrees Fahrenheit, it is necessary to store the wallboard for at least 24 hours, day and night, in an inside temperature of 55 to 65 degrees before starting application. You also want to avoid high humidity. If moisture gathers on the windows, it is too humid. Ventilate by opening the windows 2 inches from the top.

It is best to mount wallboard on the wall with the long axis going horizontally. It braces the framing, bridges any irregularity in stud spacing, reduces the amount of joint treating, and puts more of the joint treatment within easy reach. So calculate the amount you will need, and the sheet sizes, on this basis. It is better to have two 12-foot sheets going the length of a 24-foot room than three 8-foot sheets.

Mount the upper sheet first, along the ceiling, and work down. Make cutouts for windows and doors and wall outlets. Be sure the top edge butts against the ceiling panel.

To cut a wallboard panel, place it on two sawhorses with 2x4s running the length of the sheet for support. Mark the cutting line, and score the panel deeply along the mark.

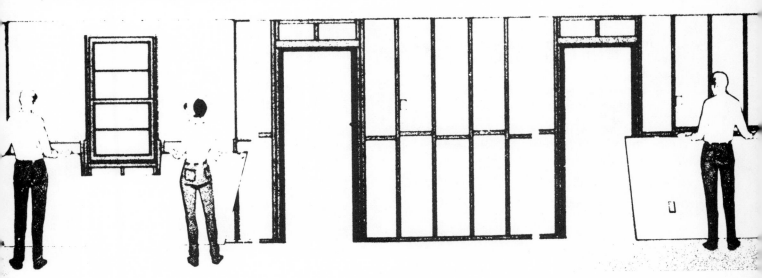

* For details on doing rough-in yourself, see *How to Build Your Own Home*, a *Successful* book by Robert C. Reschke. In particular, check chapters 22, 23, and 24.

Then lay a support under the cut, hold the panel rigid and snap it off. Then cut the paper on the other side with a knife. Smooth the edge with a rasp. To cut out a window, use a keyhole saw. For wall outlets, you'll have to drill a hole first, to get the saw in.

Be sure all joints are butted together, but loosely. Never try to force wallboard. And be sure all edges make contact with and are supported behind by a stud or other framing member. When you come to wide headers or other large lumber surfaces, don't nail the wallboard except at the edges of the lumber. You have to allow for natural shrinkage of the lumber so it won't buckle your wall.

Use coated flat head nails at 7-inch intervals to fasten the wallboard to the studs. Drive them straight in, far enough to dimple the wallboard slightly, but be careful not to break the paper.

Taping and "Spackling" Wallboard

One of the most critical operations in your entire finishing-off job will be your finishing of the wallboard in preparation for paint or other surfacing. This is the largest exposed surface in your house, and it will be obvious to everyone who visits as well as to you, so don't try to shortcut any of the steps, or speed it up.

You will need to apply three coats of joint compound, or "spackling," tape over all the joints, spackling over all nail heads. You must allow about 24 hours for each application to dry, and must keep the temperature at 55 degrees or warmer. You can mix only as much spackling as you will use at the time, because it cannot be rethinned, and when it starts to set you must discard it. Now, here are the steps:

1. Use your broad steel finishing knife ("putty" knife) to spread spackling compound into the recess left by the tapered edges of the wallboard, filling the channel evenly. Do the same over all nail heads.

2. Center the wallboard tape over the joint and press it firmly into the compound. Draw the knife along it at a 45-degree angle with enough pressure to push out excess compound and to embed the tape, but not enough to squeeze it all out. Make it smooth.

3. Wait for this to dry (24 hours) and then spread another thin coat, feathering it out a few inches in each direction. Apply a second coat to all nail heads.

4. Wait for it to dry, then apply a third coat of spackling, feathering it out another six inches. Do the same with nail heads.

5. Wait for it to dry, then sand lightly with a sanding block covered with medium grit paper.

APPLYING WALLBOARD TAPE

Next, take your wallboard tape, center it over the joint and press the tape firmly, into the bedding compound with your wallboard knife held at a 45° angle. The pressure should squeeze some compound from under the tape, but enough must be left for a good bond.

METAL CORNERBEAD

To protect corners from edge damage, install metal cornerbead after you have installed the wallboard. Nail the metal cornerbead every 5″ through gypsumboard into wood framing.

When we say do this to all joints, of course it also means inside and outside corners. You'll use tape on the inside corners, creasing it first and then pressing it into each side of the corner. But for the outside corner it is best to use a metal cornerbead for a truer, more durable corner. This is given the same spackling treatment.

Once all spackling is completed, and completely smooth, wait two more days to complete the drying; then begin further decorative treatment.

Tips on Covering the Walls

Instructions for applying wallcovering are available at stores where you buy it. But here are a few other tips that might be helpful.

Wallpaper, Vinyl or Fabric

You may choose either wallpaper or a vinyl or a fabric. Be sure to use the kind of adhesive recommended for the material. When there is a choice, synthetic adhesives are preferable to wheat paste, because they are less likely to permit mildew or to cause stains on paper surfaces.

Before cutting the first strip, open each roll and inspect for tears or defects. Hold one roll next to another to check for shading match. Once the rolls have been cut, most companies will not accept responsibility for defects.

When cutting strips to length, cut them about six inches too long, for a slight overlap at top and bottom. When the strip is up you will crease it along top and bottom and cut off the excess with a razor blade. This is more accurate than cutting the top and bottom ahead of time, because the joints may not be perfectly straight and level.

Use commercial grade single-edge blades for all cutting and trimming. They are sold at paint and hardware stores. Buy plenty of them, and throw each away after three or four cuts, because they dull rapidly.

When spreading adhesive (if rolls are not prepasted) be sure to cover the roll completely and evenly, but not too thick. A roller works better than a brush with vinyl adhesive.

Start hanging the rolls in the most-hidden corner, such as behind a door, and then go in rotation around the room. Index the pattern carefully, roll to roll. When you get around to the corner where you started, the pattern usually won't match. That is why you start in a corner that won't show.

At a window or door, do not try to use pieces. Hang the roll just as you would if the opening weren't there then cut diagonally into the corner from the open space so the paper will lie flat against the wall around the frame. Then you can crease it and cut the window area out with a razor.

It is difficult to carry a pasted full-length strip from the pasting table to the wall where it is to be applied. The simplest way is to paste half the length and then flip it back on itself, paste to paste. Then paste the other half and flip it back on itself, so the bottom end meets the top end. Carry it by draping it over one arm, then unfold the top end and smooth it onto the wall. After that, unfold the bottom end and apply it.

Fold as shown, paste to paste. If wall covering is strippable, set aside to soften for at least 5 minutes. If not strippable, hang immediately.

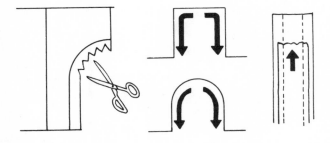

Application at arches poses special cutting problems to prevent fraying at edges. Make small cuts 1/2 in. apart so wall covering will wrap on the inside of the arch without wrinkling. Also, if you will be doing the top section of the arch, cut your strip so that it is long enough to start hanging from the inside top in the middle, and then continue down each side. The mismatch will not be seen underneath. Remember to leave 1/2 in. overlap on each side of the wall covering used underneath, 1/4 in. of which goes under the covering used on the outside. Leave 1/4 in. space between edge of arch and wall covering placed above overlap, to prevent fraying or peeling at overlapping edge. (Drawing courtesy of National Decorating Products Association).

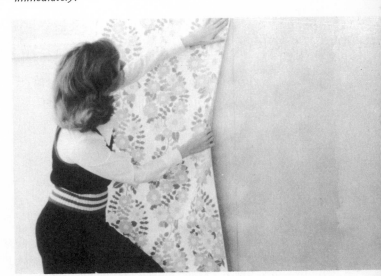

Unfold top part of strip only, leaving excess for trimming later. (Photos reproduced from Wall Coverings and Decoration, *a* Successful *book by Banov.)*

If you don't buy a special finishing brush, you can use a damp sponge to smooth the paper onto the wall. Use downward strokes, starting along the center and working out to the edges. Use a plastic seam roller to make sure the seams are tight and smooth; do not, however, use a seam roller on flocked paper.

Don't try to trim around wall outlets or switches. Remove them first, cutting a hole in the paper. Then put them back, after they have been covered with the paper, for a neat job.

Painting Walls and Ceilings

For walls that will be painted, again you will find instructions on the cans and at the store. Buy a top quality paint. You'll probably want a latex interior paint for the wall surfaces, a latex enamel for the trim. Latex materials are water-thinned, dry quickly and clean up easily.

You will do the ceiling first, the walls next, the woodwork last. When you paint the walls, paint right over the woodwork also. It will provide a good base for the finishing enamel to be put on the workwork.

Use masking tape to protect windows. Protect the floors with a dropcloth or plenty of newspapers. Remove the baseplates of all switches and wall outlets. Loosen light fixtures and let them hang down, and wrap the fixtures in plastic bags.

Mix the paint thoroughly. Thoroughly means thoroughly. Use a brush to paint a border around the ceiling. This is called "cutting in."

Use a long-handled roller for the ceiling, to avoid the risks of teetering on ladders or a makeshift scaffold. But inspect carefully as you go along, because your visibility won't be as good from this distance.

Fill the roller tray with paint, load the roller and roll it across the tray grid to remove excess, and start painting next to the already painted-on strip. Go back and forth, slow and steady, proceeding across the ceiling. If you roll too fast, the roller can sling the paint. Use cross strokes to smooth the paint.

Keep going. Don't allow a strip to dry before going on, or it can leave a streak. Do the whole ceiling without stopping.

Now to the walls. Use the paint brush to cut in along corners and around doors and windows. Cover the trim also, to provide a base for the enamel to be applied later.

If you are right-handed, start in a left-hand corner, at the top and roll up and down. Proceed around wall, always working against the wet edge, and without stopping. Roll horizontally for the smaller areas over windows and doors.

Use a sheet of thin cardboard at the bottom of each strip to protect the floor, and wipe it up immediately if you get some paint on the floor. If you should fling some drops on a window, it will wipe up easily, or scrape off easily with a razor blade when dry.

For the trim, a semi-gloss enamel is better. It is easier to clean than a flat paint. Decorators recommend that the trim be painted the same color as the walls. Apply enamel more generously but with less pressure than the wall paint. Use smooth strokes in the direction of the wood grain, and don't try to touch up a spot that has started to set.

If you want a natural finish on the trim, don't put any paint on it. Protect it from spatters with masking tape when painting the ceiling and walls.

Sand the surface and apply a coat of shellac. The shellac will dry in about six hours. Sand again, then apply a coat of gym seal. Let it dry overnight.

A reminder: Whether the trim gets enamel or a natural finish, all nail heads should be deep set and covered with putty.

Adding Moldings

Moldings — wood strips crafted into various shapes — can be used to transform plain walls into decorative accents. They also conceal cracks, and protect against wall damage. Prefinished, mass-produced moldings are relatively inexpensive, as are the metal and plastic substitutes on the market.

Standard patterns

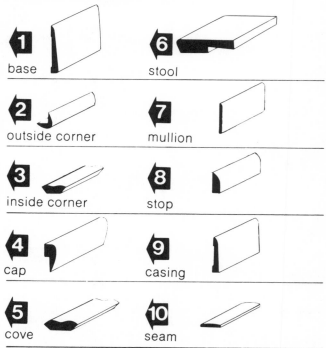

1 base
6 stool
2 outside corner
7 mullion
3 inside corner
8 stop
4 cap
9 casing
5 cove
10 seam

Standard moldings have particular applications, as shown here. Specific shapes are made prefinished and unpainted for job-site finishing. Reproduced from Finding & Fixing the Older Home *by Joseph Scram, a* Successful *book.*

With the wide variety of moldings available, you can tailor your projects exactly. No two jobs in your home need be exactly alike. (Drawings from Western Wood Moulding and Millwork Producers)

Styles and Uses

There are two major categories for moldings: functional, and decorative. A functional molding is used to cover an unsightly crack or discoloration, while decorative moldings are applied for their visual appeal alone. See the preceding page illustrations showing types of moldings.

Before and after, using sculptured polystyrene ceiling cornices for a touch of elegance. This lightweight material looks like wood once it has been painted, stained, or antiqued. (Photo courtesy of Creative Packaging Corp.)

Mitering and Coping

Mitering is used to join two moldings in a tight, 90-degree angle. This is accomplished by setting the miter box saw at 45 degrees and trimming the ends of the two moldings. For angles wider than 90 degrees, adjust and miter edges for a narrower-than-45-degree angle. For corners that are less than 90 degrees, set the miter box to an angle wider than 45 degrees.

Coping is used when one molding must butt up to the face of another molding; it is often done with cove molding. Coping can also be used to join cross-members of a complicated molding panel design, although the corners of the outer-edge molding should probably be mitered.

Instructions are given in accompanying illustrations (courtesy of the Western Wood Moulding and Millwork Producers) for transfering the profile of one molding piece to the end of the piece that will butt up to it. The drawings show a right-sided coped molding that fits the profile of a left-side butted molding in a corner. For a right side that butts into the corner, with a left-sided coped molding, reverse these steps.

Molding Application

Attaching molding is simple once corners have been coped or mitered. Corners are joined with a combination of white wood glue and brads that are nailed from the outside corners. Be sure to countersink nails below the surface, and cover with a colored putty stick made for finished moldings. Use this same countersink method for applying moldings to walls and other surfaces. In some cases, you can buy colored nails and avoid the need to countersink and cover the nails. The colored nails are tapped flush to the surface.

To miter a molding, start by cutting both ends on 45 degree angles in opposite directions.

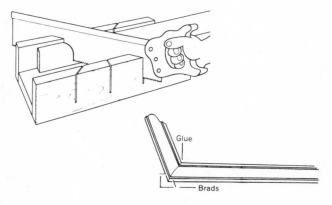

Glue the raw ends of both pieces together and secure the corner with brads.

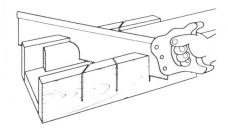

To cope a molding, make a 45 degree cut, angled so that a slanted raw edge shows from the front.

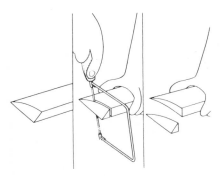

Cut straight back across the molding so that all of the slanted, raw wood is removed.

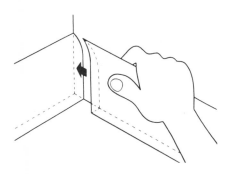

Remaining trimmed molding end will fit snugly to matching molding.

How to Apply Wall Paneling

Wood paneling is a nationwide favorite for attics and basements, and very often for many other rooms of the house. While its application usually is as a complete wall covering, it often is used on ceilings and as wainscoting (covering a lower portion of a ·wall and topped by a molding).

Paneling comes in almost every conceivable wood-grain — light, medium and dark — in soft or bold patterns and colors, or with a brick or stone appearance, or marble or butcherblock.

You'll have a choice of hardwood or softwood plywood, or hardboard (such as Masonite). Hardboard is 1/8-inch thick and is good on flat surfaces, but should not be used below grade, especially over masonry walls. Some panels are vinyl-coated for cleanability and for better wear in such places as kitchens or hallways.

Panel size usually is 4x8 feet, but they also come in 7-foot and 10-foot heights.

In looking for paneling, you'll find out quickly that there are cheap panels and there are expensive panels. We all like to save money, but think first of whether you really are saving when you buy the lower-priced materials. This is an investment, so ask questions. You will want a finish that will last for years, and you will find some warranted against de-lamination for the life of the house. Whatever price you choose to pay, look for the most quality in that price range.

You will be tempted to install paneling directly to the studs in some cases. It can be done, but it is not recommended. If direct on the studs, it transmits noise too easily and there is more tendency to warp. It is better to put up wallboard first; you will not need to fill and tape it, since it won't show. It is also safer; 1/2 inch or 3/8 inch gypsum wallboard behind 1/4 inch (or less) paneling prevents rapid spread of fire. But if you do decide to apply the panels direct to the studs, check them first for straight and true surface, shave off the high spots, and shim out the low spots. And put up building paper, plastic sheeting or some other vapor barrier to protect the panels from moisture and to add the extra insulating value of dead air space.

To find out how much paneling you need, simply measure the perimeter of the room and divide by four, as each panel will be 4 feet wide. For example, for a 16x20-foot room you'll add 16+16+20+20 to get 72 feet. Divide by four and you'll determine that you need 18 panels. But get a couple of extra panels to allow for wastage.

Major manufacturers of wall paneling offer excellent instructions on how to handle and install panels. One booklet, "All About Wall Paneling," by Champion Building Products, describes kinds of panels, shows a dozen color schemes for decorating the room with various panels, and has step-by-step installation instructions. Here are some tips from Champion.

1. Before installing, bring the material into the room where it will be placed, and stack it using full-length furring strips. This gives the panels time to adjust to the temperature and humidity in the room.

2. Walls need little preparation. On non-masonry wall, check it for a smooth, level, plumb surface, and mark stud locations on floor. You'll need wedges to hold panels 1/4 inch off floor when you install them, and they should be 1/4 inch from ceiling. Woodgrains will vary, so position all panels around room in best sequence, and mark them for position.

3. Begin paneling in a corner. Place panel there first and check for square, and mark off panel space with heavy marker. Mark imperfections that prevent panel from resting square, then trim panel to fit.

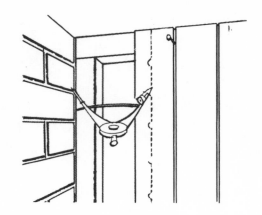

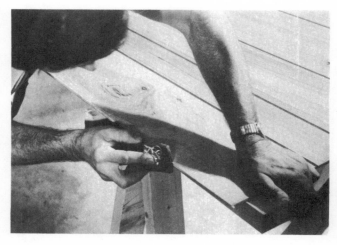

4. Plywood panels trim easily to fit into rough corners. If corner is very rough, scribe it with art compass (see drawing) and make panel conform by cutting, planing, filing or sanding.

5. You can nail panel all the way, but panel adhesive makes it easier. Apply beads of adhesive in 3-inch strips along edges, three waving beads between. Be generous with adhesive.

Paneling a Masonry Wall

Pocket-sized literature from Masonite Corp. for F-I-Yers unfolds into big sheet of step-by-step instructions. Here are some tips on installing paneling on masonry walls, from Masonite.

6. For outlet boxes, measure to edge of adjacent panel and mark area to be cut on the panel. Drill pilot holes in the corners of the space, then use a jigsaw or keyhole saw to cut area for outlet.

①

7. Mitering moldings is simple, and finishes off the room. Work clockwise around the room for measurement, mark off the molding, then cut molding in a miter box.

8. Before nailing moldings into place, compare angles for corners to check for accuracy, then nail molding to wall with brads.

1. Over masonry or concrete, use a vapor barrier of foil or plastic film. Then apply furring strips (1x2s) at top and bottom, and 16 inches on center, using concrete nails. Don't try this with an ordinary hammer. You'll need a short-handled sledge. Use 1-1/2-inch

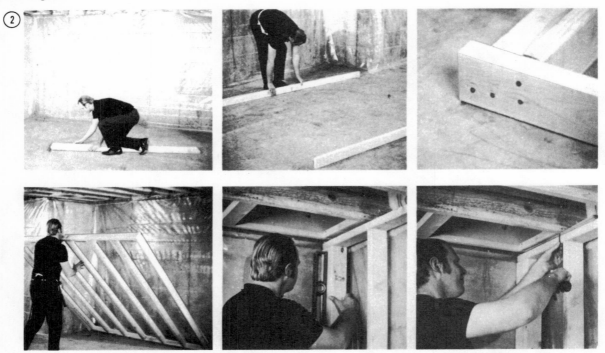

nails. And concrete nails tend to break rather than bend, so wear goggles. Check your furring strips as you go along and make sure they are plumb.

2. Many basement walls will be too uneven for furring strips, and the best way is to assemble a free-standing wall on the floor and tilt it up into position. Add a second stud where wall fits into a corner, as shown, and make wall 1/2 inch less than ceiling height for clearance when tilting into place. When you put the wall up, tack it to joist above and check for plumb.

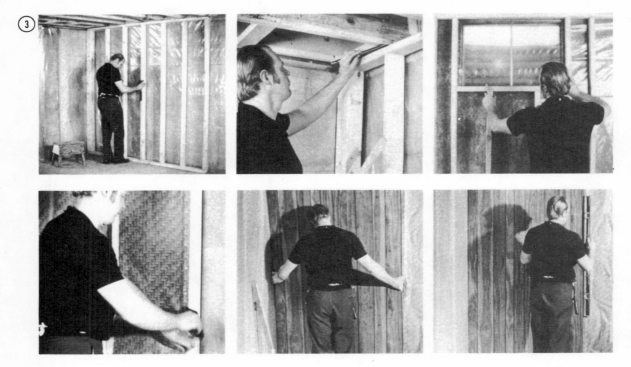

3. When it is absolutely plumb, draw a line along the floor as a guide for driving nails through floorplate (the bottom 2x4) into concrete. Use 2-1/4 inch concrete nails. But first use shingles as wedges to lift wall up tight against ceiling, and secure it there. For window openings, place studs on each side and cut studs to fit across top and bottom. Be sure wiring has been completed, tuck in insulation, and then start paneling. Remember, 1/4 inch clearance top and bottom, start in a corner, and check first panel very carefully for plumb (use a plumb bob) because this sets the pattern for the entire room.

4. Use a wedge at bottom of panel as you work, to make it easier to move and to hold it in place. A piece of wood shingle is best for this. Start nailing at corner and move down the stud. Edge nails should be 4 inches apart, and stud nails should be 8 inches apart. Edges of panels should touch very lightly. Don't force them. Mark cuts for outlets. For window openings, measure from last installed panel to edge of opening and up from floor. Check panel for fit before nailing the window area.

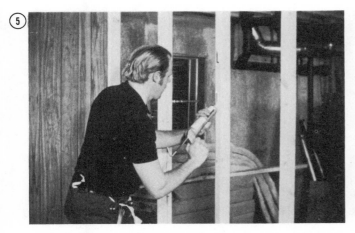

5. For partition walls where noise insulation is not a factor, you can glue panels to studs. Apply 3-inch-long beads of adhesive 6 inches apart on all intermediate studs, continuous bead at edges of panels. Set panel in place; tack it at the top; check to make sure it is properly in place; press to make contact with adhesive. Apply a uniform pressure to spread the adhesive beads evenly between the studs and the panel.

Alternatives

Another variation in panel-sizing is the "plank" type, thinner in width and 8 feet long. They are applied with adhesive and concealed metal clips to furring strips; you might find them easier to handle than the bigger panels.

Mini-Paneling by Marlite is only one third the size of standard 4x8-ft. panels. These are 16 in. side, 8 ft. high, can be handled easily by F-I-Yers with tongue-and-groove edges and concealed metal clips. ▶

All you need is two ft. of room space for this luxurious wall treatment with arched plywood panels, if you have windows at end of room (see drawing). Glass shelves hung in windows have small plants interspersed with pottery pieces, with larger plants on floor. Put fluorescent ceiling lights behind the arches for artificial sunlight when needed. Rustic effect is enhanced by roll-down bamboo shades and a Weldwood paneling with natural knots and burls. This suggestion is from Champion Building Products. Adapt for one, two or three windows.

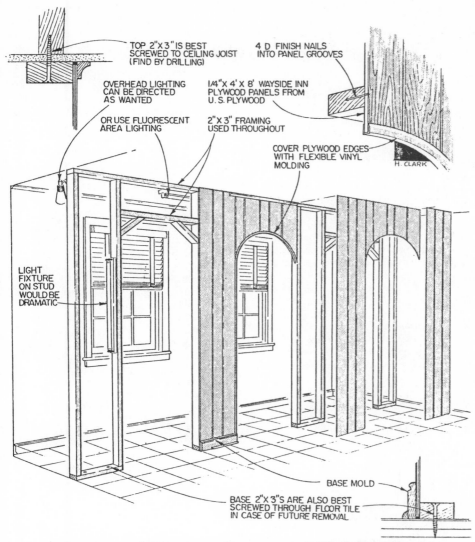

TOP 2"x 3" IS BEST
SCREWED TO CEILING JOIST
(FIND BY DRILLING)

4 D FINISH NAILS
INTO PANEL GROOVES

OVERHEAD LIGHTING
CAN BE DIRECTED
AS WANTED

1/4"x 4' X 8' WAYSIDE INN
PLYWOOD PANELS FROM
U. S. PLYWOOD

OR USE FLUORESCENT
AREA LIGHTING

2"X 3" FRAMING
USED THROUGHOUT

COVER PLYWOOD EDGES
WITH FLEXIBLE VINYL
MOLDING

H. CLARK

LIGHT
FIXTURE
ON STUD
WOULD BE
DRAMATIC

BASE MOLD

BASE 2"X 3"S ARE ALSO BEST
SCREWED THROUGH FLOOR TILE
IN CASE OF FUTURE REMOVAL

PLAN FOR ARCHED PLYWOOD WALL

Feature the window and gain storage at the same time. As long as you're doing it all yourself, why not do it right? This window wall was created by Interior Designer Abbey Darer, stores dishes, oddly-shaped appliances, lots of party items. It takes only 2 ft. from the room, is fashioned primarily of Masonite's Briarcliff hardboard paneling with bifold doors on piano hinges. The wall covering, "Little Flowers" by James Seeman, backs the cabinets so they match other walls, and takes a Joanna Western shade on the window. (See next pages for plans.)

33

Finishing Off

TURN WINDOW WALL INTO A BUFFET
(How to make the easy-to-build Hostess Storage Wall)

The wall on which this buffet was built is 11 ft. long; ceiling height is 8 ft. Materials and cutting and assembly directions are based on these dimensions.

You can easily adapt the unit to fit your available space by shortening or lengthening the center section (the two-piece serving counter and overhead display shelf). The shelf sections at each end of the unit are 32 in. wide. If your wall area is narrower than this, reduce the width to 16 in. Similarly, if the space is wide enough, you can make the sections 48 in. wide. The width of the shelf sections must be in 16 in. multiples (or within an inch or two) because of the decorative panel widths of the doors.

MATERIALS: Two 1/4 in. x 4 ft. x 8 ft. A-D plywood panels; two 1/2 in. x 4 ft. x 8 ft. particleboard panels; two 1/4 in. x 4 ft. x 8 ft. dimensional inset hardboard panels *(Masonite's Briarcliff pattern)*; 1/8 in. x 4 ft. x 4 ft. hardboard panel; 1/4 in. x 32 in. x 48 in. Peg-Board hardboard panel with hooks for hanging utensils; 36 in. x 72 in. plastic laminate panel; lumber; fourteen 5/4 x 2x8 ft, five 1x4x8 ft., 8 ft. of 1/4 in. dowel; four 14 in. heavy-duty full-extension metal drawer slides; four 48 in. shelf standards with 12 brackets; four 8 ft. lengths of continuous hinge with screws; recessed drawer pull; four wood drawer pulls; four 1-1/2 in. metal corner brackets; panel adhesive; white glue; contact cement; 6d finishing nails; 8d common nails and finishing nails; assorted flathead wood screws; white enamel; stain to match Briarcliff paneling; tarnish-resistant cloth.

DIRECTIONS—*Cutting:* For the most economical use of materials, cut particleboard and plywood according to the cutting diagrams (*see* FIG. 1) and the code below.

Code	Size *(inches)*	No. of Pieces
1/2" Particleboard		
A	15x31-1/4 overall	10
B	14x24	3
C	3-5/8x15	1
D	14x27	1
E	13x24	1
F	14-1/2x68	1
G	14-1/2x30	2
1/4" Plywood		
H	15-7/8x68	1
J	15-7/8x67-1/4	1
K	3-5/8x15-1/8	1
L	14-3/4x92-1/4	2
M	15x92-1/4	2

From the 1/8 in. hardboard, cut five 12-1/2 in. x 14 in. dividers N. Trim the perforated hardboard to 31-1/4 in. x 48 in. (O). Cut lumber as follows:
Lumber

Code	Size *(inches)*	No. of Pieces
5/4x2		
P	95-1/4	8
Q	13	14
R	29-5/8	8
1x4		
S	35-7/8	2
T	30	2
U	15-1/4	4
V	25-1/2	1
W	24	1
X	13-3/4	2
Y	68	1

Cut three 31-1/4 in. lengths of 1/4 in. dowel (Z). The decorative hardboard panels will be cut later, when all framing is in place.

ASSEMBLY: Nail together four side framing assemblies (pieces P and Q). On the two assemblies for the right cabinet, nail in additional intermediate crosspieces Q to provide backing for the dowel rods; drill three 1/4 in. holes through each of these crosspiece assemblies, as shown in FIG. 2. Set the assemblies upright and add header and base pieces R at front and back. Set assemblies in place and plumb with a level. Make sure all corners are square, then nail through framing pieces into the wall studs.

THE LEFT CABINET

In the top of one shelf A and the bottom of another, cut three 1/4 in.-deep grooves, 1/2 in. wide, spaced as shown in FIG. 2, ending 1 in. from the front edges of the shelves (the edges with the shallower notches). This can be done with a dado blade or by making multiple cuts with a power saw. If you do not have this equipment, have this operation done in a carpentry or cabinetmaking shop.

Fasten the lower shelf to the base framing. Glue three dividers B into the grooves, then glue the second shelf on the dividers and nail in place through the framing.

In the top and bottom of two more shelves A, cut five 1/4 in.-deep grooves, 1/8 in. wide, spaced as shown in FIG. 2, ending 1 in. from the front edges of the shelves. Glue spacer C in place (this piece is needed to allow the drawer to open without hitting the folding doors). Glue shelf to top of C and nail through the framing. Glue dividers N into the grooves, then glue the upper shelf to the dividers and nail through the framing.

Fasten the adjustable shelf standards to framing uprights P, flush with the inner edges. The three remaining shelves can be placed at convenient levels on the movable brackets.

THE RIGHT CABINET

In the middle of the top of one shelf A and the bottom of another, cut a 1/4 in.-deep groove 1/2 in. wide and ending 1 in. from the front edges of the shelves (*see* FIG. 2). Fasten the lower shelf to the base framing. Glue partition D in the groove, then glue the upper shelf to D and nail through the framing. Nail top shelf A in place 12 in. below the top of the unit.

Use screws or nails to attach perforated hardboard O to rear framing uprights P, directly above the intermediate shelf. Glue dowels Z in place (if the holes are too tight to slide dowels through, enlarge them slightly with a rasp).

THE PANELING

The decorative hardboard paneling must be "acclimated" to your room before use, following the directions of the manufacturer.

Masonite's Briarcliff design includes three feature strips, separating the individual rows of dimensional panels in the 4 ft.-wide sheets. Cut each of the panels as described below and in FIG. 3.

Measuring from the long edge of the hardboard that does not have a feature strip, cut a 16 in.-wide section. Apply beads of panel adhesive to the sides of the framing flanking the window and press the paneling in place.

From each of the remaining pieces of paneling, cut a strip 1-1/4 in. wide along the edge with the feature strip. Cut the remaining feature strips from the middle of the panels to a 1 in. width. Set aside the feature strips. This leaves sections 14-3/4 in.-wide (the door sections toward the middle) and 15 in.-wide (the door sections toward the walls).

FIG. 1 CUTTING DIAGRAMS FOR 4x8 PARTICLEBOARD

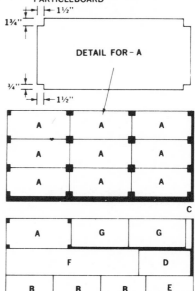

CUTTING DIAGRAM FOR 4x8 PLYWOOD

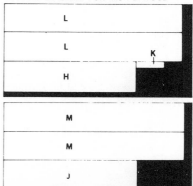

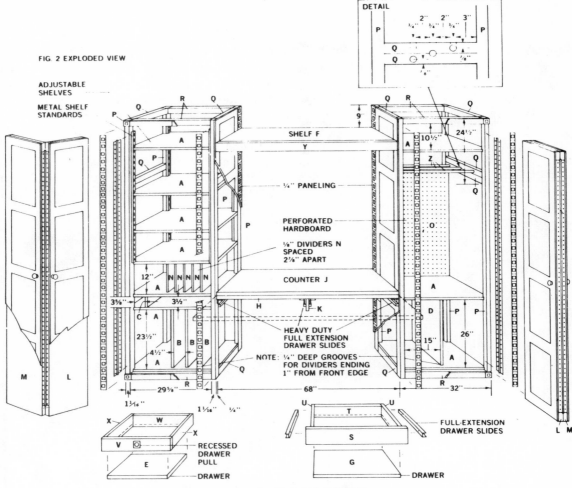

FIG. 2 EXPLODED VIEW

ADJUSTABLE SHELVES

METAL SHELF STANDARDS

SHELF F

¼" PANELING

PERFORATED HARDBOARD

⅛" DIVIDERS N SPACED 2⅞" APART

COUNTER J

HEAVY DUTY FULL EXTENSION DRAWER SLIDES

NOTE: ¼" DEEP GROOVES FOR DIVIDERS ENDING 1" FROM FRONT EDGE

FULL-EXTENSION DRAWER SLIDES

RECESSED DRAWER PULL

DRAWER

DRAWER

DETAIL

FIG. 3 CUTTING DIAGRAM FOR PANELING

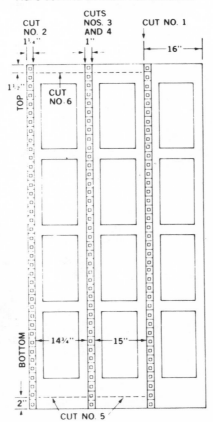

CUTS NOS. 3 AND 4

CUT NO. 2

CUT NO. 1

CUT NO. 6

TOP

BOTTOM

16"

1¼"

1"

1½"

14¾"

15"

2"

CUT NO. 5

From the bottom edge of each door panel, cut off 2 in.; set aside. From the top edges, cut 1-1/2 in. and set aside (*see* FIG. 3).

THE DOORS

Use panel adhesive to attach the panels to plywood pieces L and M. Fasten inner and outer parts of each door together with a continuous hinge (cut off excess hinge with a hacksaw).

Attach a continuous hinge to the edge of the outer section of each door. Hang the doors, with the paneling face protruding 1/4 in. in front of the framing. Glue top, bottom and side border strips (*those previously cut from the paneling*) to the framing. Attach knobs to doors.

THE MIDDLE SHELVES

The serving counter consists of two shelves stacked one atop the other when not in use. To extend the counter, the top shelf is pulled out and supported by two drawers.

The top and front edges of lower shelf H are covered with plastic laminate. The top, front and side edges of movable shelf J are also covered with the laminate. Cut the laminate and apply with contact cement, following manufacturer's instructions.

Fasten shelf H with wood screws driven through predrilled holes in the framing in the end units. Fasten center divider K to the underside of H with four metal corner braces.

Fasten top shelf F between the two end units, 9 in. below the ceiling (or directly above the window frame), with wood screws driven through predrilled holes in the framing. Nail trim piece Y to front edge of shelf F.

THE DRAWERS

Assemble each of the center drawers by gluing and nailing back T, two sides U and front S, to bottom G. Center front S so that it extends equally beyond both sides.

Install full-extension drawer slides below shelf H, attaching them to divider K and to the side cabinets. Attach slides to the drawer sides.

Assemble the drawer for the left cabinet by gluing and nailing back W, sides X and front V to bottom E. Line the drawer with tarnish-resistant cloth. Attach recessed drawer pull and set drawer in place.

Finishing: Complete the unit by staining framing members and the top shelf. Paint drawer fronts, shelves and dividers.

A Corking Good Idea might be to use natural cork as a wallcovering. This is a hand-print variety by Armstrong Cork called "Spices," imported from Spain. These are tiles, but they are easy to handle and to apply, and you find them at Armstrong Floor Fashion stores. The other picture is called "Balloonery" and is somewhat like antique copperplate engravings. Cork is different and its production is limited, and Armstrong recommends that it be installed professionally. But, with all you're going through, you may be a pro by now.

Wainscoting

Wainscoting often is desirable in a dining room or some other part of the living room, and an F-I-Yer can cut it himself to any desired height.

But Marlite offers an even easier wainscot kit. It includes ten 16x32-inch panels, all prefinished, to make a 12-foot run. Included are adhesive, installation clips and nails, and two 74-inch chair rail moldings to cap it all off. These wainscot panels have tongue-and-groove edges to make sure the panels fit together perfectly.

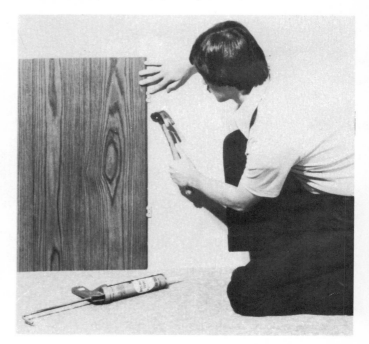

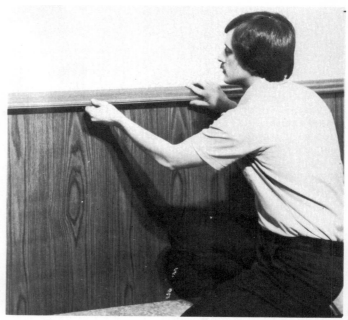

How to Lay Ceramic Tile

Many people like ceramic tile on their bathroom walls. Some like it on other walls, such as the kitchen backsplash area or on countertops or floors. This section covers countertops and floors as well as walls, so all the tile information will be in one place.

Base Surfaces

You can lay tile on any solid wall. If you should have a plastered wall, the plaster must cure for at least a month before tiling starts.

Your wallboard is an ideal surface for tiling, but it must be mounted very solidly so no movement is possible. They should be fastened to studs at 12-inch intervals.

Plywood also is a good base. But don't use interior grade plywood. It must be waterproof exterior grade.

Tools

You'll need a few special tools: A trowel notched on one side and one end, smooth on the other side and end; a small notched trowel for mixing grout and for small areas; a scriber with a tungsten carbide tip; a rubber-surfaced trowel for grouting, and a pair of tile nippers. Some tilers try to use a glass cutter instead of the scriber, but it dulls very quickly; a scriber is best.

Selection

Ceramic tiles come in several sizes and shapes. The usual tile for walls, especially for tub or shower surrounds, is 4-1/4 inches square. There are other trim tiles and corner tiles, cove base and cove base corners, and there are edging caps measuring 2 inches by 6 inches to finish it off. But some tiles come with rounded edges and can be fitted to a corner with a grout line, eliminating the need for special tiles except for the edging caps.

The little one-inch-square tiles you will see at the store are usually called "floor tiles" because that is where they are used most, although these can be used on the walls also. The best way to buy these is in mosaic sheets in which the tiles are mounted on fabric in quantities about 2 feet square, uniformly spaced for grouting.

The easiest systems to use are the "Redi-Set" sheets, which can be ordered specifically for the size of the job and which give you a number of tiles already grouted together. The sheets are numbered so that you put them up in the right sequence. The Redi-Set 100 system has 16 tiles in a sheet. The 200 system consists of the ceramic mosaics such as you might use on the floor, and the 300 system comes in larger, 7-tile squares. Each system comes with full installation instructions from American Olean.

That's the easy way. But tile is a very permanent installation and you can't change it on whim. The tile you choose will be a decorative factor in your bathroom for a long time to come. It will have to harmonize with your bathroom fixtures and other colors in the room. So you might want to choose a more exotic Mexican or Italian tile, in which case you will have to do it tile by tile, the hard way.

Tiling Your Tub

First, calculate the amount of tile you will need. Measure the two dimensions of each wall, multiply them, and you have the number of square feet for that wall. Then calculate the number of tiles you need for a square foot. For example, if you should choose a foreign decorative tile it might be 6 inches square, and you can calculate that it takes four tiles for each square foot. Get a dozen extra tiles to allow for breakage, buy it all at the same time, and check for color match.

For each 50 square feet you will need one gallon of wall-tile mastic adhesive. One pound of grout, after mixing, should cover about 18 square feet.

Now check the area to be tiled for squareness. You might find the tub is not perfectly level, or at least not square to the walls and ceiling. You will want to mark off a perfectly square area so that any fractional tiles at the corners, top and bottom will be as close as possible to the same size.

Find the lowest point of the tub. From that corner draw a level line to the opposite corner exactly one tile height above the low point. Hopefully you will find this line is perfectly square to the tub and you will not have to trim any tile, especially if you have finished the wall yourself and have set the tub yourself. You might even be able to do some minor shimming to make the tub square before you start.

Make a tile-measuring stick: a scrap of furring strip that is just about as long as the wall. Use pieces of tile to mark the stick, tile by tile; cut it off at the end so it comes out even, then place it against the wall and move it back and forth until you get it centered. Then mark the wall at each end so you will end up with the same widths for fractional tiles at each side. Draw lines on the wall to mark off the area inside the fractional tiles. This is the area in which you will put complete tiles, uncut. Tack up furring strips along the lines you have drawn, marking off what will probably be 9 near-perfect squares. The furring strips will help you align the tiles.

Spread mastic on the wall, not more than about 3x3 feet at a time, using the notched side of the trowel and pressing hard so you get even beads that are the same height as the notches in the trowel. Lay the tiles straight on. Don't try to slide them into place or you'll get mastic on the face of the tile. Go in horizontal rows, and check each row with a level before going on. If you find a tile out of place, take off all the tiles in that line and start it over, but don't use the tiles you took off until you have cleaned off the mastic.

To cut the fractional tiles for around the edges, score them with your scribing tool on the glazed side and then snap them over a straight, hard edge such as the shaft of a long screwdriver. (Or, to make this easier, see if you can rent a commercial tile cutter.)

To cut around incoming pipes or faucets, use a half tile on each side of the fixture. Mark each tile for location of the needed hole, then cut half the hole in each half-tile with the tile nippers, and fit them together around the pipe.

Let it all set for a full day before grouting. Spread the mixed grout over the surface with the rubber-surfaced trowel, making sure to force the grout into the spaces between tiles. When it starts to dry, wipe the grout excess from the faces of the tiles with a damp rag. When it is completely clean and dry, apply a grout sealer to help keep it white.

The easiest way to apply ceramic tile as a tub surround in the bathroom, is to buy it in kit form. Pictures shown here are from the Redi-Set system by American Olean. Since you need not make the interior square first, there is not as much cutting to do.

1. Redi-Set ceramic tile tub surround is packaged in two cartons, consists of eight sheets of tile pregrouted with a flexible, waterproof, stain and mildew-resistant silicone grout. Included are internal corner strips, tile for the tub "leg", and four extra tiles.

2. Draw a vertical line in middle of back wall and horizontal level line 55-1/2 in. above tub. Also draw a vertical line 32-1/2 in. out from back wall as a guide for spreading adhesive.

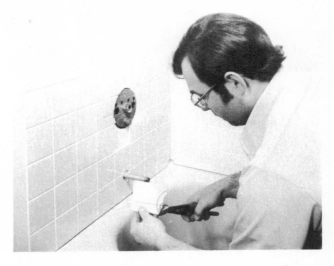

5. Use nippers to cut holes for pipe. Clean grout from edges of tiles and replace in sheets.

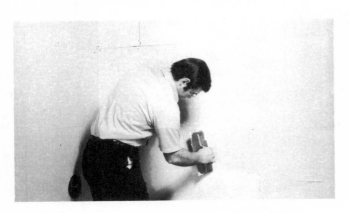

3. Apply ceramic tile wall adhesive on back wall using notched trowel. Use enough pressure to lines of adhesive are even, and be sure you can intermittently see the lines you drew on the wall.

4. Set sheet No. 1 at lower left corner, minimum of 1/8 in. above tub, within the guidelines drawn. Install remaining sheets 2, 3 and 4 on back wall. Then spread adhesive and apply sheets 5 and 6 on one end wall and sheets 7 and 8 on pipe wall.

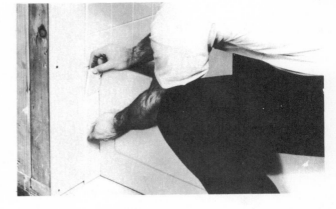

6. Cut tile legs to proper width by scoring along straight-edge with glass cutter and nipping along score line with nippers. Outside edges of this tile are glazed so no trim is necessary.

7. Peel surface paper from pressure-sensitive adhesive on the back of corner strips and apply strips to tile sheets. Align internal corner joints with side-wall joints.

8. *Grout joints between the sheets, at tub line and corner strips, with grout gun filled with same silicone rubber which was used to pregrout the sheets. Nozzle on gun is made to conform to joint.*

9. *Caulk with same material around pipe-holes.*

10. *Clean as you go. Joints may be smoothed with finger after spraying with denatured alcohol. Excess silicone rubber on face of tile can be cleaned by going over joint with cheesecloth saturated with alcohol.*

11. *Completed tub surround looks neat and professional. In this photo, home owner went on to do floor with same material.*

12. *Here's another example. Redi-Set was used as a wainscot and floor, and fabric was used above for designer effect.*

13. In another example with contemporary look, tile counter covers heating inlet and has white vinyl cushion on top where you can lie down and get a tan from sun lamps above.

14. Another decorating suggestion is this plaid pattern. There are all 4-1/4-in. tiles, but the colored ones are scored at the factory for decorative effect.

Now You Can Tile a Countertop

Now that you know so much about ceramic tile, you might want to consider the California-type countertop in your kitchen. The West-coasters like ceramic tile.

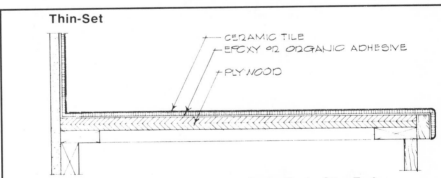

Thin-Set

CERAMIC TILE
EPOXY OR ORGANIC ADHESIVE
PLYWOOD

Recommended Uses:
- on countertops where thin-set method is desired.

Requirements:
- 3/4" exterior plywood base required.
- the bottom edge of the countertop trim must be set the proper distance above the finish floor material to allow clearance for dishwasters, compactors, etc.

Materials:
- epoxy mortar — ANSI A118.3-1969.
- organic adhesive — ANSI A136.1-1967. Type I for prolonged water resistance.
- grout — specify type (see Pages 6 & 7).

Preparation by Other Trades:
- when tile is set with epoxy leave 1/4" gap between sheets of plywood. Apply batten to under side of sheets to cover gap.

Preparation by Tile Trade:
- when tile is set with epoxy completely fill gap between sheets of plywood with epoxy.
- prime surface before applying organic adhesive when recommended by adhesive manufacturer.

Installation Specifications:
- adhesive — ANSI A108.4-1968.
- epoxy — ANSI A108.6-1969.

You can use plain or highly decorative tile. You even can use Redi-Set. But you must watch the measurements.

Your kitchen countertop has to come out far enough from the back wall to cover the cabinets and extend a bit over them. That's 25 inches. And it has to be built up 1-1/2 inches from the top of the cabinets, because many ranges now have lips that extend over the countertop, and they are a fixed height.

So build up the countertop with 3/4-inch exterior grade plywood. Lay out your tiles physically, allowing for grout, so you can check the sizes of the border tiles front and back, and at either end. Cut the border tiles.

If the countertop is long and you use more than one sheet of plywood, leave a gap of 1/4 inch between sheets. When you lay the tile, fill this gap with epoxy. Use a batten on under side of sheets to bridge the gap.

You can use the same type of silicone adhesive for the kitchen top as you used in the bathroom.

When you get the countertop laid, do the same vertically with the backsplash area. Usually the tile is taken all the way up to the wall cabinets. The ideal way to do this is to apply the tile to the wall first, if you are going to tile the entire wall. Then you shim up the space behind where the cabinets will go and hang the cabinets over the tile. Then as the house settles you do not end up with gaps where the tile line would meet the cabinet line.

How to Install a Corian Tub Surround

Man-made "cultured" marbles can be beautiful in the bathroom, on any walls, or as tub or shower surrounds. They come in a wide range of marbling patterns and colors.

But one of these, DuPont's Corian, is unique (at the time of this writing, at least) because it is workable with ordinary household tools. It can be drilled, sawed, planed or cut, although it is much more limited in colors and patterns than other cultured marbles. It comes in cameo white, or with faint green or beige marbling, in 1/4-inch thickness for wall application.

You can buy a bathtub wall kit that has all the needed materials and complete instructions. The photos below and on next page show how it goes up.

1. As with any other task, read instructions fully, until you understand every step. Open the kit and trial-fit the panels around the tub enclosure. This will show which end panels should butt against wall, or against back wall corner panels. You have a leeway of 1/4-in. in positioning end panels.

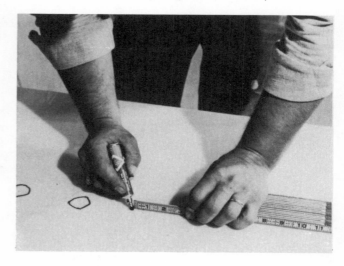

2. Remove handles, faucets, etc. if they are in place, measure the position on the wall of all projecting fixtures to get the location of holes that must be made in Corian.
3. Mark the needed openings on Corian with pencil.

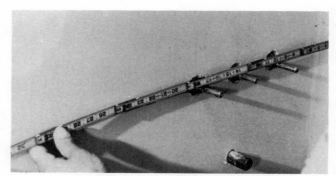

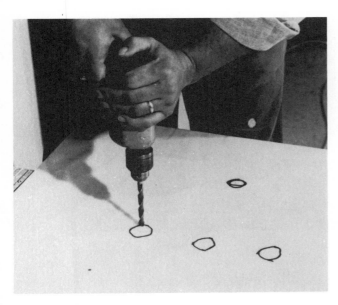

4. Drill small holes in each opening to be cut. Drill along edge of circle, not in middle.

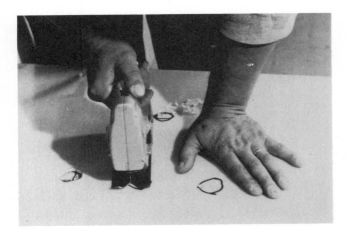

5. Use a saber saw to cut holes about 1/2-in. bigger diameter than the diameter of each fitting.

6. Measure area to be covered with Corian and mark it with pencil, as a guide for applying adhesive that comes in your kit.

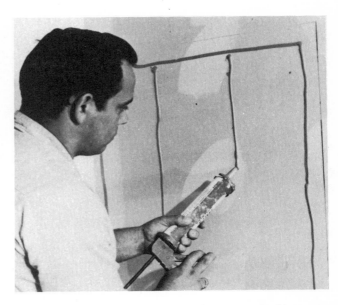

7. Apply adhesive, running beads across top and bottom, four beads from top to bottom about 6 to 8 in. apart, and run a bead around each plumbing opening.

8. Install Corian sheet within seven minutes after applying adhesive, pressing firmly to make sure of good overall contact. After positioning, pull panel away from the wall for two minutes to allow adhesive solvent to vent. Leave slight gap at bottom for caulk.

9. After positioning the Corian, drive in two or three 6-penny finishing nails under the sheet to prevent it from slipping down. You need a slight gap here for caulk, no more than 1/8-in. Install the other end panel in the same way.

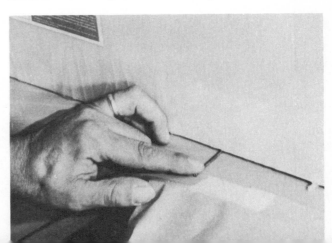

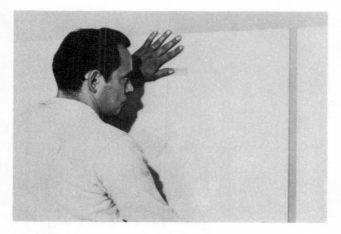

10. *You'll have two panels left, back wall corner panels. They'll go on the back wall, close in to the corners but with a gap between. Apply adhesive, running beads across top and bottom and four beads from top to bottom just as you did the end panels. Put up one panel at a time as you did the end panels, with nail shim as before. If you have cut a soap dish opening, or any other opening, run a bead around the opening.*

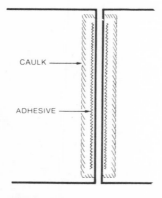

11. *You will have left a back wall center strip. Mark vertical lines at the gap in the back wall, using level to be sure you get them straight and even. Apply adhesive and caulk, as shown.*

12. *Press on the back wall center strip, pressing firmly into place, and then smooth caulk bead with finger.*

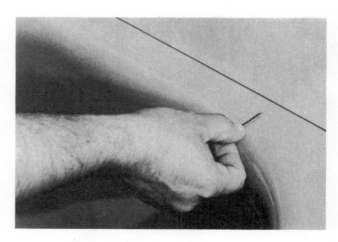

13. *Remove shim nails from under panels.*

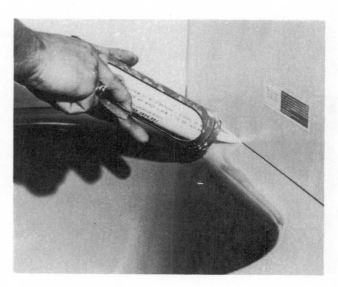

14. *Caulk the opening between panels and tub. When you do this, hold caulk tub at 45-degree angle and push, so caulk is ahead of tube. This pushes caulk into gap.*

15. *Caulk corners where panels meet in the same way. Run a bead of caulk along top of panels, along sides of back wall center strip and outside edges of end panels. Then smooth all caulk seams with damp sponge.*

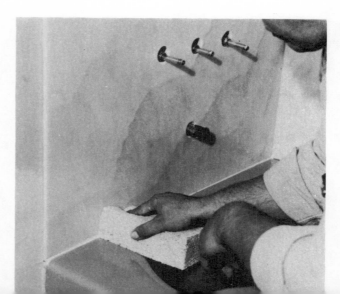

16. *Finished tub surround of Corian.*

6. Ceilings: Looking up can be great, no matter what your outlook is

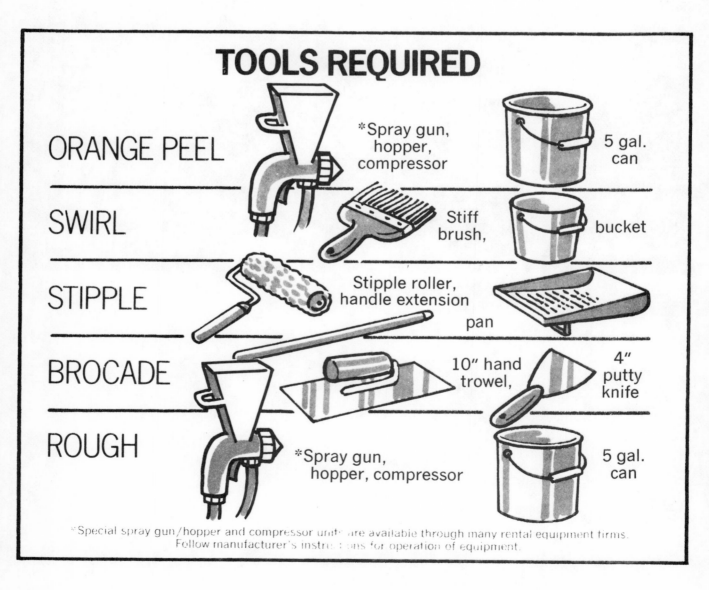

TOOLS REQUIRED

ORANGE PEEL — *Spray gun, hopper, compressor — 5 gal. can

SWIRL — Stiff brush, bucket

STIPPLE — Stipple roller, handle extension — pan

BROCADE — 10" hand trowel, 4" putty knife

ROUGH — *Spray gun, hopper, compressor — 5 gal. can

*Special spray gun/hopper and compressor units are available through many rental equipment firms. Follow manufacturer's instructions for operation of equipment.

There are several ways to finish ceilings, from simple painting to installation of lightweight ceiling tiles for the main living areas of the house, to suspended ceilings or wood paneling in finishing-off basements or attics. Ceiling tiles, if tongue-and-grooved, can be installed directly to bare joists if they are perfectly even. They seldom are perfectly even, however, and it is usually easier to install gypsum board ceilings over the joists first, to make sure the ceiling is flat and even.

If the joists are bare when you take delivery on your new home, apply the wallboard to the ceiling before you finish the walls. The directions are the same as in the chapter on walls. To help in handling the unwieldy sheets, first make a "T" of scrap lumber slightly longer than the height of the room, to wedge up one end of the sheet as you apply the other. You'll need a helper for this, and it is tiring, so don't get careless or try to hurry it. Place the panels across the ceiling framing, stagger the end joints, and butt all sheets loosely without forcing.

Paint

Light color is important when finishing-off the ceiling, either in paint or ceiling tile. In paint, it is good to use the same color as the walls because then there is less of an overlapping problem. In any case, the ceiling should not be darker than the walls or it will make the room seem smaller. Use a flat latex.

Remember, light colors reflect light and make the room seem larger. Cool colors seem to move away from you, while warm colors seem to advance toward you. If you don't have professional decorating help, white is always safe.

Get a top-grade paint, and stir thoroughly to work the pigment up from the bottom of the can. Use a brush to paint a strip two or three inches wide around the room, then use a roller with an extended handle so you can paint from the floor. It is safer and less tiring. Roll in slow, even strokes. Heavy pressure can cause bubbles or spatters.

You Also Can Try Texturing

Texturing is another way to paint. For textured walls you use different materials and, sometimes, different equipment.

The various textures are roughly classified as orange peel, a texture like an orange; swirl, which looks like sweeping arcs this way and that; stipple, a sort of smooth roughness; brocade, with heavy overlaps; or rough, which looks like stucco.

For orange peel, swirl, or stipple you will use a regular wall texture. It will say that on the package. For brocade you can use wall texture or Georgia-Pacific's Ready-Mix Joint Compound. For rough, use polystyrene ceiling texture.

For either orange peel or rough texture, you apply with a spray gun. Most rental equipment firms have spray gun/hoppers and compressor units for rent. And you'll need a 5-gallon can for the material.

You use a stiff brush and a bucket for swirl. For stipple you use a roller. For brocade you need a 10-inch hand trowel and a 4-inch putty knife.

Make a "T" of scrap lumber to support sheetrock panels for ceiling installations. It should be slightly longer than the floor-to-ceiling height.

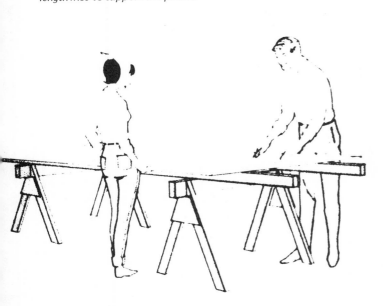

When cutting sheetrock use sawhorses, with 2x4 boards laid lengthwise to support the panels.

Coverage of these materials varies greatly, according to the texture and the application method. As an example, Georgia-Pacific's "Denswall Wall Texture" comes in a 25-pound bag and will cover 200 square feet if applied with a trowel, 400 square feet with a roller, or 1,000 square feet if sprayed. G-P's "Ready-Mix Joint Compound" comes in a 5-pound can, covers 200 to 300 square feet with roller, trowel or brush, or with a sponge which often is used for creative swirl textures. G-P's Polystyrene is sprayed, comes in a 32-pound bag and covers 300 to 400 square feet. G-P also has an instruction booklet you can write for, called "Do-It-Yourself Wall & Ceiling Texturing."

Use of texture does not eliminate the need to finish off your gypsum board joints properly. They still must be taped and finished smooth first. It also is good to paint the entire surface with one coat of latex primer before texturing.

Wallpaper

Putting wallpaper on ceilings introduces physical problems, mostly those of endurance and flexibility.

Remember that ceilings should always be hung first; you should if possible have another person help you, even if he does no more than hold the material while you stand on the ladder or scaffold, and work the material into place.

First, put up a plumb line, using tacks to hold the cord. To make this easier, use two ladders and put an extension plank between them to stand on. This improvised scaffold will only put you a foot or two above the floor, and will mean less ladder-moving and less danger.

Since you probably will be putting up a pretty long strip, usually longer than the 8-foot wall strip, fold it carefully. The ceiling strips can be folded the usual way, or in a special accordion fold that is particularly convenient. Each folded section should be at least one foot long (see photos).

Dimensions

In measuring for ceilings, allow for one-half-inch overlaps for all adjoining walls. That means the top and bottom of the strips need these allowances — a total of one inch for each strip — all across. Also, the two end strips need a half inch each for their edges to overlap onto the walls they meet.

For example: if you have a narrow dimension of 11 feet, each strip should be at least 11 feet 1 inch long. If the longer dimension is 19 feet, then have enough strips to cover 19 feet 1 inch, allowing one-half inch overlap for the sides of the end strips.

Begin hanging at the least noticeable corner or ceiling area.

For papering ceilings, an accordian fold is needed for the extra-long strips. Fold sections so that pasted side always faces pasted side, with each section at least a foot long.

How to Install Ceiling Tiles

Acoustical tiles, or ceiling tiles or panels, can be used anywhere in the house. They are a common choice for basements, where they can be suspended from the joists above and hang low enough to hide piping, ductwork and the like. They come in "systems" that have a variety of light fixtures that match.

Tiles can be cemented directly to the joists, which usually will result in a very uneven installation. In such cases, use furring strips. They can be cemented directly to the wallboard on the ceiling.

If you use wood furring strips, nail them up 12 inches on center, or mark off a grid 12 inches by 24 inches for the panels. You'll have to use about 260 nails for the furring on a 12-foot by 12-foot ceiling, and that's a lot of nailing. Tiles can then be stapled to the furring. Wood furring is somewhat expensive and is subject to warping. Armstrong has developed what it calls its "Integrid" furring channel method, which uses metal furring strips that need only one nail every 48 inches and will not warp.

For gluing tiles to a wallboard ceiling, use a latex adhesive such as Elmer's Latex Ceiling Tile Adhesive, or another brand marked for ceiling tile. Put four small dabs of adhesive in each corner and one in the center of a square tile and press it into place. Too much adhesive will make application uneven.

If you select tiles that are slotted to butt together perfectly, you don't have to worry about laying it out and making the border tiles match.

But some tiles have beveled edges or designs and patterns that make it necessary to lay them out and cut tiles for even borders. Here's how to go about it.

First, measure each wall. You'll have to do this anyway to figure how much tile you'll need. Multiply the length of the ceiling by the width to get square feet, and that's how many tiles you'll need, plus border tiles, if you use the 12-inch by 12-inch tiles, or half that number if you use 12-inch by 24-inch tiles. These sizes are fairly standard for residential use, although Armstrong's Chandelier ceiling tiles come either in 12-inch squares or in pieces 12-by-48 inches.

Now to calculate the size of the border tiles, disregard the feet in your measurements and take only the leftover inches. Add 12 to the number of inches and divide by two, and that gives you the size of the border tile you will have to cut. For example, if the ceiling measures 12 feet and 4 inches along one axis, add 12 to the 4 inches to get 16, divide by 2 and you get 8 inches for the size of the border tiles at each end. If the other dimension for the ceiling is 9 feet 2 inches, add 12 to the 2 inches and you get 14. Divide that by 2 and you get 7 inches for the border tiles on either side.

Recheck your figures to make sure. Then cut the border tiles and install them all the way around. Then start in a corner and lay full tiles, first one way, then across, stapling or gluing as you go. If you are stapling, you'll find that some of your border tiles have no staple tabs because you cut them off in cutting the border tiles to size. Nail them with the nails, close to the walls where they will be hidden by the molding you will put up to finish the job off.

For cutting the tiles, you can use a fine-tooth saw or a sharp utility knife. Saw the tile face up.

One other thing: If you want acoustical tiles, be sure to read the labels; some give sound benefits and some do not. Also, some are flame-resistant. Good acoustical tiles will absorb up to 70 percent of the noise striking them.

Suspended Ceilings

Selection

In suspended ceiling systems, panels are normally 2 feet wide and 4 feet long. Some panels are glass fiber, such as CertainTeed. Some are polystyrene, such as Leigh. There are other materials. Armstrong has woodgrain ceiling planks that are 4 feet long with a choice of three different widths: 8-3/16 inches, 6-5/8 inches or 5-3/16 inches. To any of those widths you must add 11/16 inch to allow for the stapling flanges. But Armstrong says you can simplify, for measuring purposes, to 9, 7-1/2 and 6 inches respectively; this will allow for the stapling flanges.

All of these systems also have light-diffusing panels to go under lighting fixtures. Armstrong has special light fixtures for its ceilings. You can make your entire suspended ceiling luminous if you wish.

In short you have a lot of choices here, so do some investigating to make sure you get what you want.

Installation

To install a suspended ceiling, start with a chalk line around the perimeter of the room at the height you want the ceiling. Be sure you allow room under the joists and under ductwork, because panels will have to be angled in above the grid system and lowered into place. Check the chalk line for level before snapping it.

Nail the metal wall angles to the walls at the chalk line. Then calculate your border tile sizes. Since you are using panels measuring 2 by 4 feet, you simply divide the length of the room by 4, then divide what's left over by 2 and that's the size of your border tile on the long axis. The other way, divide the width of the room by 2 feet, then divide the remainder by 2 for the width of the border tiles.

What you are going to do now is lay out a grid system, using main "tees" and cross "tees". This grid will hang from the existing ceiling which, in a basement, means from the joists. You'll hang it with wires from the screw eyes you'll put in the joists, for insertion into holes in the tees that are provided for this purpose. Then you will simply angle the panels up into the grid system and lower them into place.

Install the main tees first, 4 feet apart. These come in 12-foot lengths, and you'll cut them to the right length with tin snips. The cross tees are 4 feet long, and you will twist them into place at 2-foot intervals provided in the main tees, to complete the grid system.

A representative suspended ceiling looks this way when you look up at it. Note that the suspending members are visible, and for esthetics you should have border tiles at opposite ends or at sides match. In this small ceiling, only the center tiles are the full 2 by 4 ft. in size. You must be sure to put the cross tees at 90-degree angle precisely from main tees. Armstrong makes luminous ceiling fixtures that fit exactly to replace and full tile, but you must figure that in first and wire it. An advantage of this system in basements is that tiles can be lifted out easily to get at wiring, piping or ducting that is concealed. An excellent booklet on how to do it is available from Armstrong, called "How to Install Ceiling Tile, Suspended Ceilings and Lighting Fixtures." For other literature, write Borden Chemical for "Elmer's Guide to Installing Ceiling Tile" or to Leigh Products for a leaflet on "Suspended Ceiling Kits." (For addresses, see Manufacturer Index.)

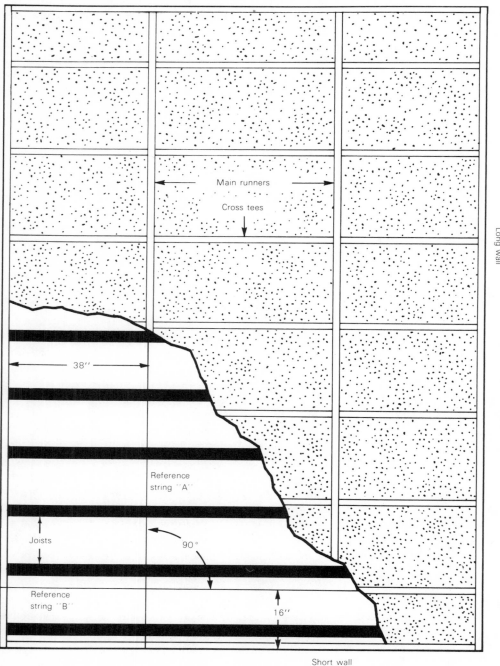

To start the first main tee, measure the width of the border tile out from the wall angle you have put up. Mark the spot, and run a string from that point across to the opposite, already-attached wall angle. Put the screw eyes into the joists above this line, hang wires from the eyes, and bend them at the string. These wires will hook into the main tee and support it. The wires do not have to be in exact intervals, since they will not be visible and you do not need a lot of them; the whole system is very light. You'll see a lot of holes in the tees, but this is just to give you plenty of leeway when hanging the wires vertically. A wire roughly every three feet will be plenty.

Install the rest of your main tees, moving the string in each case to be sure you bend the wires at the right point for a level ceiling.

For the first cross tee, again measure out the length of the border tile and snap in the cross tee. Then continue at 2-foot intervals.

Before tilting the panels into place, use a pair of pliers to flatten the bends in your wires. Otherwise it will be difficult to lay the panels into place in the grid. Where you have difficulty, hook your fingernails into the tee at the point where the wire is obstructing the panel, and push the tee away so the panel can drop in.

Easy Ceiling Without Wires

The accompanying photos show how to install an Armstrong Integrid system, which doesn't use wires.

1. The Armstrong Integrid system has interlocking butts so you need not worry about border tiles. To start, nail wall angles 2 in. below ceiling, all the way around.

2. Then nail metal furring channels direct to ceiling. The first is placed 26 in. out from wall, others are then placed 4 ft. apart. They take a nail every 48 in.

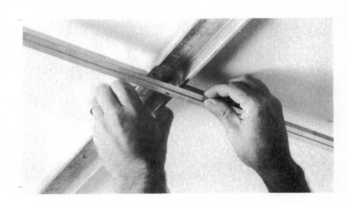

3. Integrid cross tees are designed for easy installation. Just bend the sides of the channel inward slightly and clip it in.

4. When all furring channels are in place, lay in first tile on the wall angle, clip a 48-in. cross tee onto the channel and slide the tee into a concealed slot on the leading edge of the tile. Here, installer is using Chandelier tile, 12-in. by 48-in.

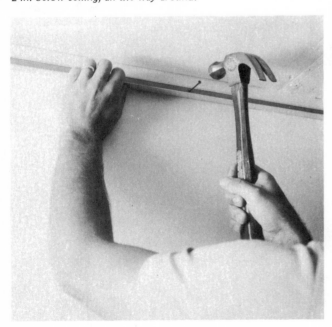

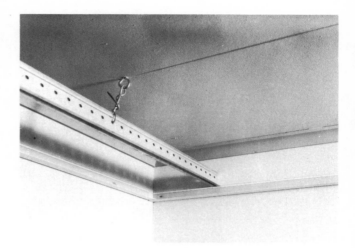

5. Continue across the room installing tiles and cross tees. At the end of a row, when tile needs to be cut, use a sharp utility knife; then use the leftover to start next row. Note that all supporting members are concealed.

6. Same system can be used on Armstrong's Decorator Chandelier tiles, which are 12 by 12 in.

7. You also can use Integrid system with hanger wires to drop ceiling lower. The first runner is always put 26 in. out, with remaining units every 48 in. on center, perpendicular to the direction of joists.

8. The finished ceiling forms a continuous pattern, whether dropped 2 in. or suspended from hanging wires.

7. Floors: How to cover them, from hardwood to resilient to carpeting

An unfinished home usually is delivered with a subfloor installed. This consists of 1x6s or 1x8s laid diagonally across the joists. You have some choices from this point on, but whatever you do, check first that the subfloor is down tight.

Selection

Your choice now is whether you want hardwood floors or some sort of wall-to-wall floor covering, which might be carpet or resilient tile or sheet tile. Resilient sheet goods comes in several types, often called "linoleum," but linoleum has not been made in this country since 1974.

Vinyl Sheet Flooring

The two standard sheet types are vinyl and vinyl-asbestos, the latter being somewhat less expensive. The four principal types of vinyl floors are rotovinyl, in which the patterns are produced by a combination photographic-printing process, making them very realistic in simulating certain textures (for example wood parquet); inlaid vinyl, in which the design extends all the way through and which usually looks richer and deeper than rotovinyl; through-color vinyl, a newer technique that permits shimmering, translucent colors, very durable; and no-wax, which has a tougher-than-vinyl surface that shines without wax.

All rotovinyl floors have an inner layer of foam cushioning. The others might or might not be cushioned. The finest quality no-wax floor will be most expensive, then inlaid vinyl, but a rotovinyl with exceptionally thick cushioning will cost as much as an inlaid vinyl. You will also pay a premium for the adhesive-backed place-and-press tile, but this is by far the easiest floor to install. It costs no more than the least expensive sheet floor.

Carpeting

Wall-to-wall carpeting can cut the noise level in your house by 50 percent. It costs a little more than hardwood flooring, but it adds comfort and value to the house.

The eight basic types of fibers used in the manufacture of carpet each have special properties and often are sold by trademark names adopted by the manufacturer. No one fiber is best for all purposes, and carpets frequently are made from a combination of fibers.

Here's a brief rundown on the various fibers:

Nylon. Used in nearly half the carpeting made in the U.S., has good resilience and excellent wear resistance, good colorfastness and is priced from $5 to $12 per square yard.

Polyester. Has about a fifth of the carpet market, soft and luxurious appearance for living rooms and bedrooms, good wear resistance and colorfastness. Priced from $7 to $15 per square yard.

Acrylic. Used for about 12 percent of all carpet pile fiber, has a soft appearance, good resilience, colorfastness and wear resistance. Priced from $7 to $14 per square yard.

Modacrylic. Generally used with acrylic fibers to increase flame resistance. Has fair to good wear resistance and moderate resilience. Priced $7 to $14 per square yard.

Wool. Has declined in use since advent of man-made fibers, gives soft, warm appearance, excellent resilience and good resistance to showing soil and wear. Prices $10 to $28 per square yard.

Polypropylene. Also known as "olefin," principally used for indoor-outdoor carpeting as it has excellent resistance to moisture, water-based stains and is highly colorfast. Priced $4 to $10 per square yard.

Rayon. The least expensive man-made fiber, usually found in bathroom and scatter rugs, has poor resilience and fair resistance to wear and stains. Many rayon rugs are washable. Priced $4 to $9 per square yard.

Cotton. Usually found in scatter rugs, has poor resilience, good wear resistance and fair soil resistance. Like rayon, may be washed. Priced from $4 to $10.

Government regulations require that a carpet label must show the percentage by weight of each fiber in blend combinations and less than 20 percent of any fiber would not be enough to affect carpet and quality and should be looked upon as chiefly a selling point.

There are a great variety of carpet textures, including level loop pile, cut pile or plush, level tip shear, multilevel loop, random shear, sculptured or carved, shag, and frieze or twist.

Underlayments

If you are not installing hardwood floors, you will need an underlayment to go over the subfloor and under the carpet or resilient flooring. This might be 3/8-inch plywood or fiberboard or 1/4-inch hardboard or particleboard either 1/4 or 3/8 thick. Purpose of the underlayment is simply to give you a good, smooth surface for the flooring. You'll buy it in sheets, or panels, and nail it to the floor joists through the subfloor, making sure not to let the under-layment joints come close to the subfloor joints.

Hardwood Floors

Laying hardwood flooring looks like a big job, but it is relatively easy. You can make it easier by renting an automatic nailer.

First, you will sweep the subfloor very clean, making sure there are no protruding nailheads. Then lay a rosin paper over the subfloor. You will want to lay your floor across the joists, not in the same direction as the joists, and absolutely parallel with the walls. You might be using something exotic, but the usual hardwood floor material will be 3/4-inch oak, tongue-and-grooved and in random lengths. Usual practice is to use them as they come from the package, alternating long and short lengths but, of course, using the short lengths for inside closets.

After laying the floor, finish it by first applying a paste filler, wiping the surplus clean before it hardens, then a coat of shellac which you will let dry for six hours, and then a coat of gym seal; let seal dry overnight.

Oak in random lengths, 3/4 in. thick, is a popular material for hardwood floors. You start with a layer of rosin paper laid over the subfloor — just laid, not nailed or glued — and then lay flooring across the joists. Start at an outside wall and work your way across the room.

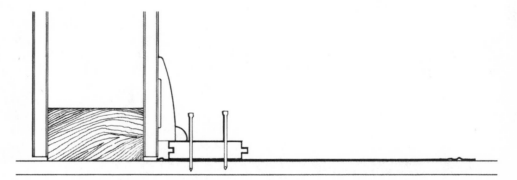

1. Start first board perfectly parallel with wall and about 3/16 in. from the wall, with the groove side toward the wall. Nail straight down through the board into the joist. Drawing shows positioning of board and molding you will apply when finished.

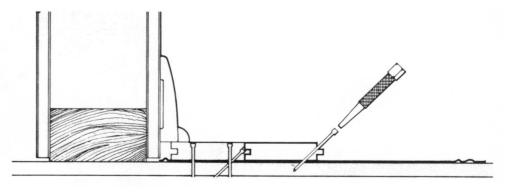

2. As you lay subsequent boards, nail them at 45-to-50 degree angle across the tongue of the board and sink them with a nail punch. Nails should be 2 in. in from each end, no more than 16 in. apart, and into joists whenever possible.

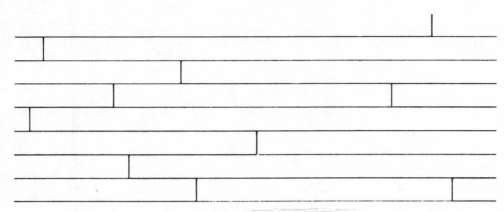

3. Boards will come in all lengths. Stagger them. Use them as they come from the package, without ever having two joints together. Use shorter boards in closets and in center of room where carpet will hide them.

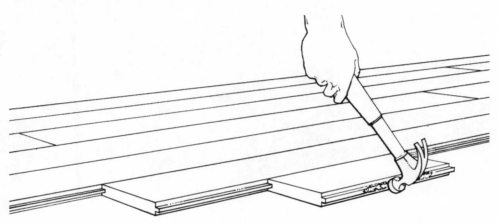

4. Use hammer to tighten each board to last row as you go, but don't hammer directly on floor board. Use scrap.

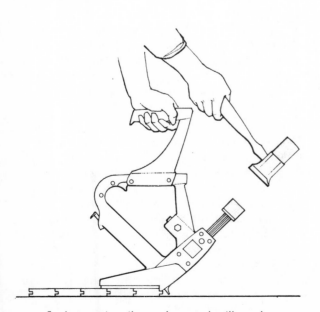

5. Automatic nailer can be rented, will save hours.

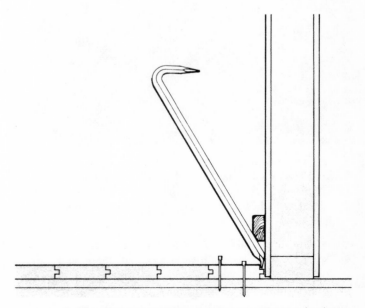

6. Use pinch bar to tighten last board, with scrap lumber to protect wall. Then sand with the grain.

Installing Wall-to-Wall Carpeting

Use a floorplan, with room dimensions marked, to plan for size and colors. On the first floor you probably would want the same color throughout open areas, but you might want a different color in first-floor bedrooms or other rooms. You probably would want different colors in upstairs bedrooms, but think it over carefully because it's pretty permanent.

You will want to buy carpet for the area, padding to go under it, and tackless strip to go around all perimeters. Padding protects the carpet as well as making it feel more luxurious. Tackless strip is a specially designed plywood 1/4 inch thick and an inch wide; it comes in 4-foot lengths and is fitted with zinc-plated steel pins that protrude upward at an angle of about 60 degrees. You install the strip around the walls, then stretch the carpet over the strip, hooking it securely.

The accompanying photos show how Ridge Homes recommends the installation job be done:

1. Be sure all baseboards are painted first, as the carpet edges will be tucked down against them.

2. Install tackless strip around the walls. The strip comes with nails prestarted; you just have to hammer them down. Position the strip slightly away from the wall to leave room for the carpet edge to be tucked down. This distance from the wall will depend on the thickness of your carpet (not including padding) and you want it fairly tight. Don't install strip across doorways, just around walls.

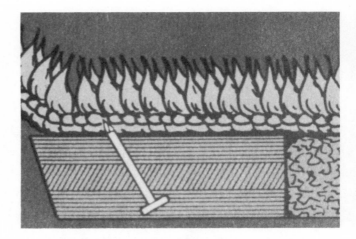

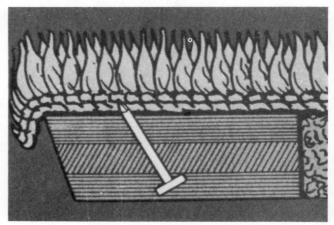

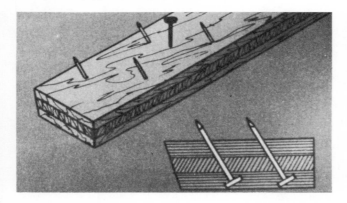

3. Lay the padding inside the strip, right up against it. Staple it to floor where edges come together, staples about 8 inches apart, then every 6 inches around the perimeter.

4. Unroll the carpet and spread it over the entire area. Where pieces come together, stitch them with an overcast stitch. Reinforce the seams with tape and then iron them with a seaming iron.

5. To start hooking the carpet, lay the trimmed edge over the strip along one wall and about 3/8 inch up the wall and, compressing it that way, push down to get the inside row of pins hooked into the carpet backing. Then tap it lightly with the hammer or run the hammer back and forth in an ironing action to get all tacks engaged. *Don't push this edge down into the gully at the wall yet,* or it will come unhooked. Don't start pushing the edge down until the carpet is hooked on the opposite wall.

6. Now you'll start stretching, using your knee-kicker. You have one corner securely hooked. Notice the drawing. With corner A hooked, stretch along wall A to B and hook corner B. Then go back to corner A and stretch along wall A to C and hook corner C. Then stretch and temporarily hook corner D along wall C to D. Now to back to corner C and stretch, using the carpet-kicker, to corner D. Finally, if you have any surplus carpet along wall A to C, trim it flush with wall, leaving a little to tuck down into the gully behind the tackless strip. (See opposite page).

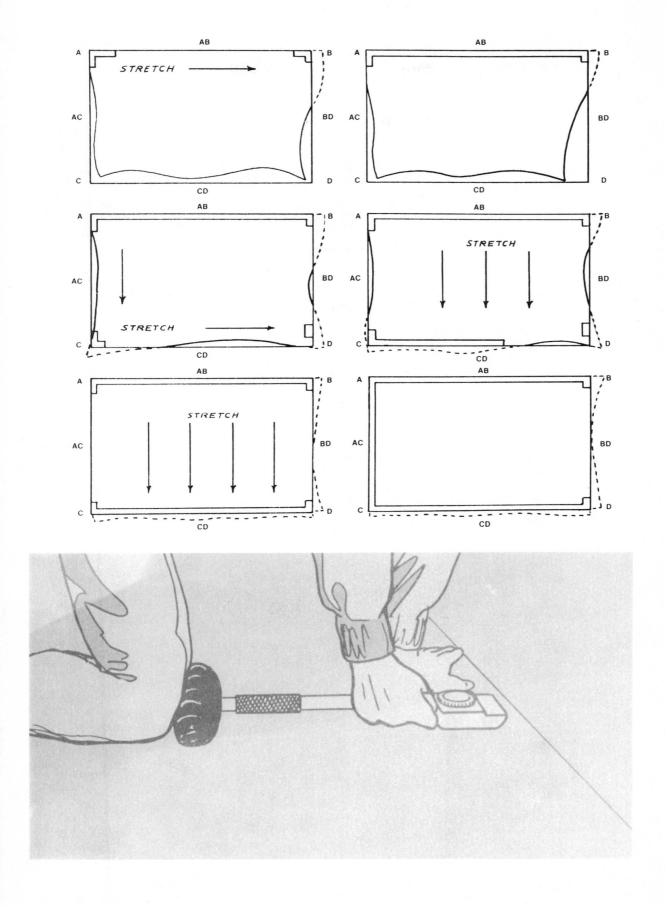

Next install wall A to C on the strip using the technique we described, and you have the two sides and one end done. To finish, start at corner D and go to B to complete that end. Now you can tuck the lip down into the gully at the wall, all around.

In using the carpet-kicker, note the adjustable head with teeth that extend at an angle. These teeth should grip the backing of the carpet, but must not go completely through and reach the padding underneath. You work on your knees, grasping the neck of the kicker with your right hand, bumping the kicker once or twice with your knee and then holding it there. Your free hand holds the previously kicked carpet so it is not disturbed by the kick.

7. Use a metal molding strip at doorways. This is made for the purpose, to conceal the edge of the carpet and prevent tripping. The molding has two rows of teeth which hold the carpet. Rough-trim the carpet up to the molding, leaving about 1-1/2 inches of excess. Use the kicker to kick it up and use a hammer and chisel to chisel the carpet into the lip of the molding. Then use a rubber mallet to fold down the lip over the carpet.

Shag Carpets

If you like shag carpet, it is much easier to install and it needs no stretching. Shown here is a sequence recommended by Armstrong Cork Co.

1. First, run a chalk line around the perimeter of the room, leaving marks on both the floor and the wall.

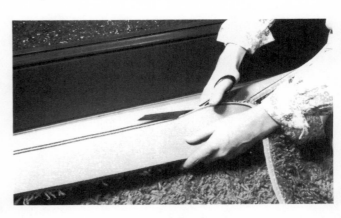

2. Lay out the carpet with any excess running up the wall. Then press firmly into the floor-wall joint so the chalk marks will be transferred to the carpet backing. Cut with heavy shears, between the two lines, for a perfect fit to room.
3. Use 2-sided tape to tape down at seams and doorways.

4. *If more carpeting is needed, just roll it out beside what you already have installed and press down at seam on the tape.*

Carpet Squares

Carpet squares are very easy to install. Some have patterns that must be fitted together. Others, like this Armstrong style called "Feelings," is a saxony plush with a built-in self-stick foam backing. The design fits together at random; just press into place.

Installing Vinyl Flooring

Cushioned Vinyl

Cushioned vinyl floors are easy following the directions given in these steps from Congoleum.

1. *Butt one edge against straightest wall, allowing 3 extra in. on other three sides. Then from there, use ruler or carpenter's square to push down tight and trim at wall.*
2. *Make a "relief cut" at corner where excess laps up both walls, so flooring will lie flat for fitting.*

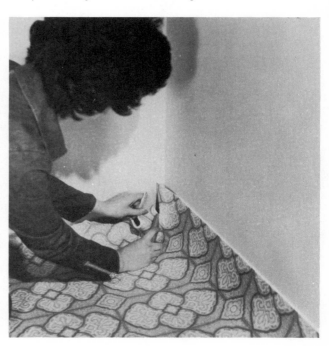

Complicated Installations

For a more complicated installation, where you must fit pieces around cabinets and closets, you'll have to take careful measurements and mark all of them on a floorplan. Then transfer them to the material (this is Armstrong's no-wax floor) in another room where it will lie flat, and cut there. Then take it back and apply adhesive to half, as noted before.

3. After it all is cut to fit, apply foam adhesive to half of floor surface and unroll new flooring back onto wet adhesive. Flatten with a pushbroom.
4. Roll up the other side and repeat.

This no-wax floor from Armstrong (Premier Sundial) is installed with staples to hold it in place; no adhesive is needed. Quarter-round molding is used to hide staples.

8. Basement use can double living space; or, how to upgrade life below grade.

Finishing off the basement is one of the most-delayed activities in the home. And this is most regrettable, because the basement represents a vast amount of living space adaptable to general family living. But "below grade" is what makes it a bit different from other areas in the home: it is below ground level, which causes a few problems.

Basement Troubles

The problems are humidity, moisture, condensation, bugs, the need to select materials accordingly, and a collection of unsightly pipes, ducts and wires.

All of these can be easily solved.

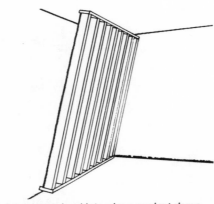

2x3 frame wedged into place against damp or masonry wall.

First step for basement walls, after solving moisture seepage or leakage problems, if any, is to make the masonry walls workable. You can attach furring, using concrete nails. But the best way is to build a new wall of 2x3 lumber on the floor and tilt it into place, wedge it tight and nail securely to ceiling and to concrete floor. Use a vapor barrier between new wall and masonry wall (see Chap. 5).

Water Problems

Leakage through a crack in masonry wall or floor can be solved by undercutting the crack and filling it with hydraulic cement. Use a hammer and chisel to cut into the crack so it is smaller at the surface than below surface, which will lock the cement in place. This cement sets fast, and any incoming water helps it set.

Seepage is water that works its way in through the pores of the concrete. Solve it by coating the interior walls with a waterproofing compound. The root of this problem lies in too much ground water outside the basement wall; you must do something to reduce that excess water or the waterproofing will not work. To cut down on that outside water, make sure your ground surface slopes slightly away from the house. Check to see that downspouts don't dump the water right at the walls. Make sure your gardens or shrubberies don't trap the water right at the wall where it goes straight down.

Condensation is common in basements. It results when normal humidity in the air comes against the cold masonry walls or cold pipes. You then find drops of water collecting. Use vapor barriers to insulate the walls, add a ventilating fan to circulate the air, and buy a dehumidifier. The vent fan should go in one of the attic windows. Other moisture comes from condensation on the pipes. Wrap them with insulating wrap made for the purpose.

Bugs

Bugs will tend to disappear as you correct the moisture problems. Select insecticides for bugs that remain. Once you make the basement tight and relatively moisture-free and get rid of bugs, this space will be as usable as other areas in the home.

Pipes and Ducts

Unsightly ductwork and pipes are easily hidden with suspended ceilings, and partitions around the heating plant and water heater.

Materials and Plans

Even with these problems solved, you will want to use materials suitable for below grade. Some are not, so check all labels carefully and consult with your builder or supplier. (See Chapter 5 on wall paneling.)

Here's a typical basement stairway, which might look pretty hopeless at first. The improvement work already has been started with framing on the wall and insulation between.

Here's another unfinished area of the same basement.

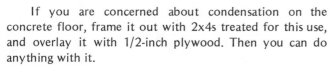

Now look at the difference. Marlite paneling was used on the walls and to hide area under stairs, with an access door for that storage area. Suspended ceiling was added to hide the mess above.

These two views show the changes that are possible. This is one big room, so same flooring and Marlite planking are used throughout. Windows are shuttered; ceiling is dropped where necessary to hide joists.

If you are concerned about condensation on the concrete floor, frame it out with 2x4s treated for this use, and overlay it with 1/2-inch plywood. Then you can do anything with it.

This is the biggest unbroken area of your home, so plan what you want to do with it first. Sketch out the floorplan accurately, marking locations of windows and wall offsets, of furnace, water heater, laundry appliances if they are there. Then make a dozen copies of the floorplan so you can play around with it. Try the ideas in this chapter, or check all of the "home" magazines for ideas before you settle on anything.*

If you plan a game room, make sure you allow space for table tennis or pool table or whatever you like. If you will have a laundry here, expand the idea and make it a "housekeeping" room with provisions for sewing, ironing and other home activities. If you are going to partition off the mechanical segment with furnace and water heater, make a room big enough to store out-of-season clothing where it will also be out of sight. Be practical — don't be captivated by a new idea, such as a basement bar, if you will really do all your entertaining upstairs.

This space is all yours. Make the most of it.

Shown is another typical basement. This is what a basement inevitably deteriorates to in only a few months if left unfinished.

There's little resemblance to a basement in these three photos of the finished versions. Armstrong's Chandelier suspended ceiling, which hides the hanging strips, was used. Luminous panels were placed over the bar at left. Box beams enclose a steel post at bar. There's a dining nook in background at right, desk area at left.

The photo opposite shows other end near desk area, with fold-up ping pong table and open pegboard storage wall with overhead fluorescent illumination. Floor is cushioned vinyl, also by Armstrong.

Another view of the other part of this basement family area shows electric fireplace, with vinyl floor covered with Armstrong area rug. Stereo system and television flank fireplace. All of this is in a basement measuring 22 ft. by 31 ft; this basement design was featured in an issue of Family Circle *magazine.*

* Additional ideas and specific instructions can be found in *Successful Family and Recreation Rooms* by Jane Cornell.

We are so close to our own homes that sometimes we don't realize how much better we could make them if we tried a little harder. When we are doing all the work ourselves, it is too easy to settle for "good enough." In the following series of photos, we'll show you what seemed good enough to one F-I-Yer, but how it was then improved by an A.S.I.D. designer, Ethel Samuels. The basement featured here measures 33x25 ft.

▲ *With floor and walls covered, this family room was relatively comfortable but had a "downstairs" look.*

But a new emphasis on walls and ceiling took away the downstairs look. Samuels used Masonite's hardboard paneling, Armstrong's Chandelier ceiling and Juno carpeting, added built-in shelving, brought out the piano as a design feature, gave new life to old furniture. Base cabinets from the "before" wall units are used as end tables. ▼

A beautiful desk loses its detail in half-finished setting.

Here the desk is brought out where it shows. Ceiling is dropped with Chandelier tile, laundry units are hidden behind pillars and arches faced with Masonite paneling. (For tips on making that archway, see Chap. 5.)

There's the former utility area at the left, now obscured by the arches shown in previous picture. Now about these stairs . . .

. . . Here the ceiling is dropped, the stairs are enclosed all the way and dressed up with new steps-to-ceiling balustrade. Balustrade is made from mitered strips of same Masonite paneling used to enclose stairs. Door opens to sewing room under steps.

The former view down the steps, to drape-hidden storage area, definitely indicates a basement.

But the basement became a "lower level" when that droopy drape was replaced with this live-plant display, and a cabinet in the former storage area.

Another was used to conceal the water heater at the end of an unfinished wallboard wall (furnace is behind that wall).

Wall benefits from paneling to create concealed cabinetry for built-in bar, TV and stereo centers, and record collection. Hinges at left are for access door to water heater.

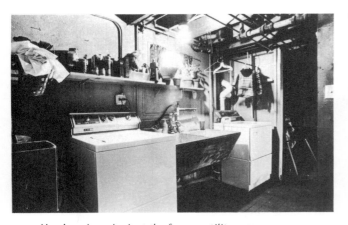

Here's a closer look at the former utility area.

This is the same utility area, with laundry behind the arched wall, along with furnace. But space around it has become a pleasant sitting area.

Original play area was large, but perhaps not conducive to play.

And the back of the original play area was a disaster of retired furniture and unsightly laundry. Note delivery door.

Here playroom has been finished off in a style that youngsters can enjoy. They have a place for homework, snacks, crafts, reading. Walls are covered with a stucco-like Masonite paneling; plywood portholes outline the windows; floors are Armstrong Quiet Zone vinyl.

Another view of playroom shows back wall. The catch on the wall at upper right is about all that shows now of that delivery door. View to left again shows the laundry area, with shade partially up.

This family wanted nothing more from the basement than one big party room for big groups. The important thing is that they finished it completely, with wall paneling and bar made from the same panel pattern, flooring and finished ceiling with recessed lights.

Here's the room at bottom of stairs set for a party. Stairs are at left. Sliding doors to bedroom (right) and walls use Masonite Coach House paneling. Tables slide away and this room serves as workshop as well as sewing center.

Three photos (above and at left) show a 20x30-ft. basement converted into a hobby/sewing/entertainment center and a bedroom for two boys. Here, the two bottom steps of the stairway were turned into the room, but a pass-through was created as part of a design to hide sewer pipes and to also make it easy to carry long lengths of lumber from upstairs into the workshop.

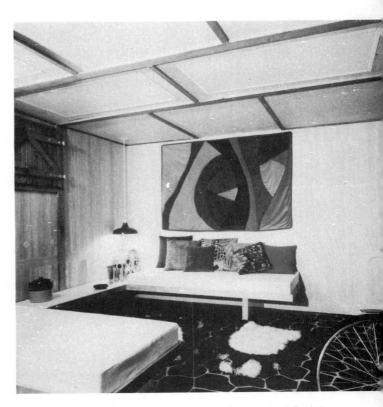

Here's the bedroom for two boys, with couch beds built-in, covered with 5-in. foam mattresses covered with denim slip covers. Window is shuttered for either sunlight or privacy. Not showing in picture are two built-in closets and two sets of bookshelves.

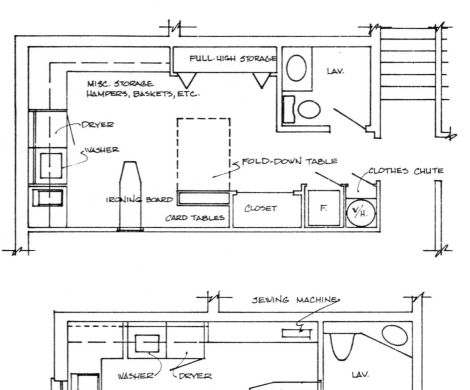

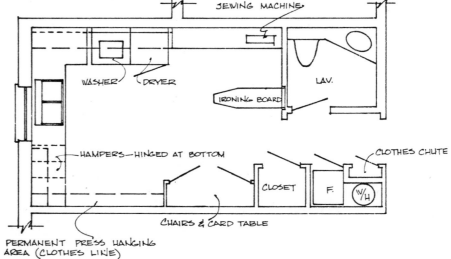

HOUSEKEEPING ROOMS

Laundry areas might go anywhere in the house, but the basement often provides the most usable and adaptable space for a laundry area with multiple functions.

William Ketcham, CKD (that stands for Certified Kitchen Designer), has designed thousands of these for home builders. Ketcham calls them "Housekeeping Rooms" because of the many functions he thinks properly belong there. Here are three of his full Housekeeping rooms, plus other smaller laundry areas for more limited space.

Ketcham suggests that all of these can be adapted to available space, but there are features that should be included in a Housekeeping Room. It should be a complete laundry facility for soiled clothes, storage, washing, drying, ironing, storage for supplies, and sewing center. There should be shelves for stacking dried articles, a closet for sorting baskets to separate delicates, colors, rough, etc., which can have a door or be open for easier access. It should have a pull-out rod for hanging permanent press and freshly ironed articles, a short clothes line for nylons and permanent press, a sewing center with fold-down table for dress pattern layout and cutting and with shelves for all sorts of sewing needs, a bulk storage closet for card tables, chairs, large vases and other odd-sized pieces, and storage of seasonal items such as Christmas decorations.

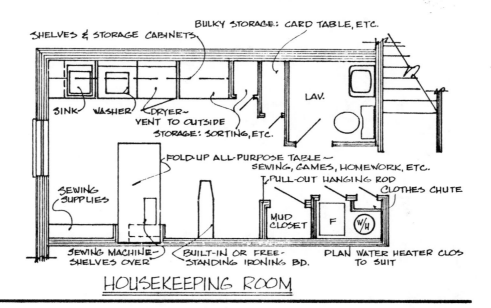

SHELVES & STORAGE CABINETS

BULKY STORAGE: CARD TABLE, ETC.

SINK WASHER DRYER~
VENT TO OUTSIDE
STORAGE: SORTING, ETC.

LAV.

FOLD-UP ALL-PURPOSE TABLE~
SEWING, GAMES, HOMEWORK, ETC.

PULL-OUT HANGING ROD

CLOTHES CHUTE

SEWING
SUPPLIES

MUD
CLOSET

F

W/H

SEWING MACHINE~
SHELVES OVER

BUILT-IN OR FREE-
STANDING IRONING BD.

PLAN WATER HEATER CLOS
TO SUIT

HOUSEKEEPING ROOM

THIS IS A MINIMUM AREA AND CAN BE DEVELOPED
AND EXPANDED TO SUIT THE OWNER'S NEEDS AND
WORKING HABITS. (WE FEEL THAT ALL LAUNDRIES
SHOULD HAVE A SINK FOR DUTIES DONE OUTSIDE
THE AUTOMATIC WASHER.)

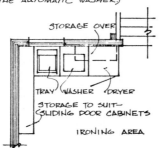

STORAGE OVER

TRAY WASHER DRYER

STORAGE TO SUIT~
SLIDING DOOR CABINETS

IRONING AREA

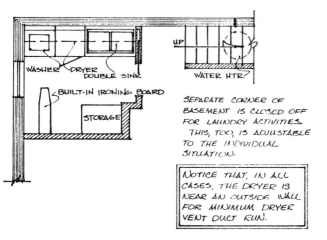

WASHER DRYER
DOUBLE SINK

BUILT-IN IRONING BOARD

STORAGE

UP

WATER HTR.

SEPARATE CORNER OF
BASEMENT IS CLOSED OFF
FOR LAUNDRY ACTIVITIES.
THIS, TOO, IS ADJUSTABLE
TO THE INDIVIDUAL
SITUATION.

NOTICE THAT, IN ALL
CASES, THE DRYER IS
NEAR AN OUTSIDE WALL
FOR MINIMUM DRYER
VENT DUCT RUN.

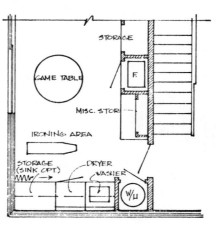

STORAGE

GAME TABLE

F

MISC. STOR.

IRONING AREA

STORAGE
(SINK OPT.)

DRYER

WASHER

W/H

LAUNDRY HERE IS PART
OF A BASEMENT GAME
ROOM — CAN BE
CLOSED OFF TO KEEP
THE WASH OUT OF THE
PARTIES.

BASEMENT LAUNDRY AREAS

Here is a bare-minimum laundry area with hamper for soiled clothes, GE's Dispensall washer system, cabinets for necessary storage, and bifold doors can close it off.

Where there is really a space problem, Ketchum suggests this installation, which still provides hanging area and storage area. This is the only dryer designed for inside exhausting (Hotpoint). In all other units, you must be sure to locate dryer as near as possible to outside wall for venting.

An exterior hardboard siding (above) was used imaginatively with an oak grain hardboard paneling, both from Masonite, in this basement. The center divider conceals support posts, and separates billiard area.

Opposite corner of the same basement (below) was finished off with a bar and the same Bayside lap siding. But this is a family bar, not an entertainment bar, and behind it are a small range and under-counter refrigerator to make it a satellite kitchen.

Softwood plywood was used to create this arched wall and to decorate the rest of interior with the warmth of wood. Note how this F-I-Yer included built-in storage in walls. (Photo by American Plywood Assn.)

Standard kitchen cabinets (these by Boise Cascade) were used to finish off this room with ample storage space. Notice they even are used as base for the bed.

Builder left the second-floor ceiling off (rafters were painted by buyer) at buyer's request, so this bright room could be made using low, shallow attic space that would have been unusable. Designer Peg Walker did the room in bright Riverdale drapery fabrics, some of them glued to the Stauffer windowshade cloth, with a Begelow Fortrel run brought up to seating, and with Micarta plastic laminates.

Laundry in basement doesn't have to be dull. Here sink-front was made in orange, as were two of the storage drawers, contrasting with light-colored washer and dryer. All was constructed of plywood.

Kitchen cabinets can be built easily into storage walls. Some companies provide framework, but if not it is easy to build for open shelving spaces.

Yes you can — this modernistic kitchen was designed by Hotpoint, but, futuristic as it looks, a handy home owner could duplicate it. Black and white surfaces are made of Textolite plastic laminate, which can be bent as shown when heated with a heat-gun. Seams where the sheets join are along top sides where they don't show. Appliances are all standard, and you can make the shapes with plywood.

This attic was made into a complete kitchen by Hotpoint designers, and it could be done in other attics where self-sufficient living quarters are desired.

This attic was fully insulated between rafters and on outside walls, then covered with Weldwood paneling from Champion Building Products. A series of platforms were built to eliminate need for furniture, and to provide bed, work area, dining area, seating and storage.

You can add genuine brick and genuine ceramic tile floor to add character to your new kitchen. Here brick was used to make cooking alcove. Tile is American Olean's Birch Andorra.

Opposite end of room shows more use of knotty pine for kitchen cabinets, in all a very unconventional finishing-off job. The floor covering is Martinique cushioned vinyl by Congoleum.

This first-floor room was finished in natural wood with bamboo squares on the ceiling and knotty pine that need no painting. Fireplace corner is real brick.

In the sometimes strange configuration possible in an attic, particularly if the upstairs ceiling has been left off, you can get an interesting bathroom such as this. This is an American Olean Tile photo showing how a design motif can be inspired by something natural, in this case a willow tree. There's a mirror at the right, beside the shower framing, that seems to extend the room, and "skylight" windows added horizontally for daylight.

You'll see these two pictures in black and white in the chapter on basements. This shows you how much color can add to creative ideas in a children's playroom. And notice the children's art is part of the color. Masonite photos.

Decorating becomes another creative task in finishing off. Here the owner made a very simple window framing, duplicated it with the same molding along the ceiling, and painted it the same brown to match window shades. Shades are "Calcutta" by Graber, and color is picked up in table cloth and patchwork bedspread. Flooring is Congoleum's Cushionfloor, "Fairhaven" pattern.

If you have a view as nice as this, kitchen and eating area can be arranged along the outer wall to take advantage. Casement windows admit plenty of light and give best view for meal preparation area as well as informal dining counter. That's a glass cooktop at the end of the peninsula (Amana) with a Corning "Counter-saver" next to it for putting down hot pans. Floor is ceramic tile with textured surface, chestnut color, by American Olean.

You'll see this picture in black and white in the kitchen chapter, showing how you can do a kitchen yourself and even incorporate a laundry (the tall, red thing at left, with dryer above and washer below). This shows how color can be a real decorative factor, the bright red contrasting with paneling by Champion International.

When you are doing the finishing off, take time to be this creative with windows (floor-to-ceiling) and with dropped ceilings, as over the sofa. This is a Champion International "idea room" upstairs, with paneling applied to furring over the framework.

Glass above in this sunbelt home really brings the outdoors indoors, but wouldn't be practical in the north. With this openness, the bright colors go well, including the light-colored paneling used even to encase the beams. Champion International photo.

This is a basement playroom, all of it below grade below the windows. And it may be hard to conceive this when you are looking at bare concrete and uncovered joists, but that's when you have to start. Note the built-in play area at the windows, and the sleep area; to preserve the decor as a theme you must have the window shades matching major items in the room. Photo by Window Shade Manufacturers Assn.

Creative playroom includes play equipment, bunk beds, study area and bright cheerful colors in this basement. Hardwood flooring was added on 2x3 framework and plywood subfloor, and otherwise whole room was made from plywood, painted. Champion International photo.

Weldwood paneling by Champion International was used to create this basement living room. Note the built-in storage framing the sofa, "down" lights installed in beam that hides duct, and the contrast of vertical installation on outside walls and horizontal installation on partition.

"Candyland" is the name of the paneling used to create this youth's room in an attic. Window was added in gable space for more daylight, and bed was made as a storage area. Champion International photo.

Attic joists stayed exposed, but dressed up, in this added bedroom made livable by decor. Windows aren't real, but harmonizing fabrics there, on the walls and in bedspread, make a pleasant room. Note also how steps were used to create a raised sewing area. Photo by Window Shade Manufacturers Assn.

Don't be afraid to aim for a great kitchen. You might not have space for this one (above), but it can be scaled down. These are stock cabinets, Heirloom by IXL, and they are not cheap but they are far from the most expensive. They come in modular sizes so they can be fitted into any room. Check the chapter on kitchens first, so you know how to plan this in.

9. Attics: Space is limited, but you can do a lot with a little

First step in any attic always is to insulate. Champion Building Products plywood paneling was laid over this insulation job to retain attic roof look.

Attics are as various as the builders who build them. Some have a lot of living space available to owners who want to finish them off. Others have none. Many builders can offer optional dormers, which increase the living space. Generally, you can't consider it living space if the height is less than 7 feet floor-to-ceiling.

Most often you will find you can create one room by dropping partitions from rafters to joists, and prepare the floor with 1/2-inch plywood as a subfloor.

But whenever you do, don't block off the peripheral space entirely. It is great for storage, so you will want access to it.

Comfort

Other than its shape, cut by the slope of the roof, the problem with any attic is that it is very cold in the winter and very hot in the summer.

Insulation

You know the answer to that problem — insulation. Any attic should be insulated even if it is not to be lived in. Insulation will save energy year-around.

If it will not be finished off, at least insulate the entire floor of the attic.

If you will create a room there, insulate well between the rafters, and insulate the walls you erect. And even though it will cost more in insulation, there are many who believe it best to insulate the entire shell of any attic, including the space that won't be used.

Ventilation

However much you insulate, your attic will still need ventilation. If you are keeping it entirely open and creating a room there, you will add windows that can provide ventilation. But if you are putting up partitions to create a living space, you will have to provide ventilation both for the new room and for the other spaces under the roof that will trap heat in the summer and cold in the winter.

The trapped heat, if unvented, will transfer into the other living areas of the house and cause your air conditioner to work harder, costing you more money every summer, indefinitely.

Trapped cold in the winter will similarly transfer and put more load on your heating system. In addition it will cause condensation of moisture on the underside of your roof sheathing and rafters, leading to serious deterioration in time.

Good insulation will slow this process. But it can't stop it.

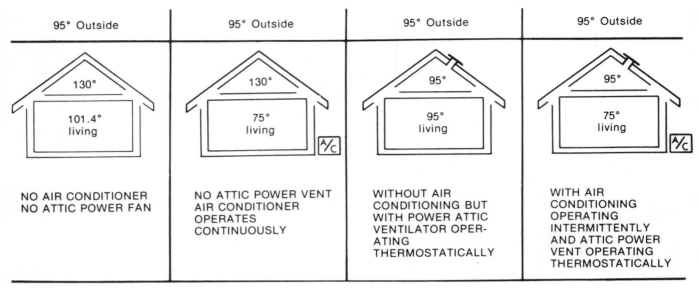

95° Outside	95° Outside	95° Outside	95° Outside
130° / 101.4° living	130° / 75° living [A/C]	95° / 95° living	95° / 75° living [A/C]
NO AIR CONDITIONER NO ATTIC POWER FAN	NO ATTIC POWER VENT AIR CONDITIONER OPERATES CONTINUOUSLY	WITHOUT AIR CONDITIONING BUT WITH POWER ATTIC VENTILATOR OPERATING THERMOSTATICALLY	WITH AIR CONDITIONING OPERATING INTERMITTENTLY AND ATTIC POWER VENT OPERATING THERMOSTATICALLY

Proper ventilation can greatly reduce the temperature of your superheated attic (Leslie-Locke).

Vents

You have a choice of various forms of "static" venting, or power venting. The builder usually will have built in some screened or louvered vents in the soffit of the roof (the underside of the overhang) and possibly he will have installed louvered vents at the peaks of the gables. This helps, but it isn't enough to provide the air changes that will remove heat in the summer and cold-plus-condensation in the winter. To do that efficiently, you would need almost continuous soffit vents plus a vent running all along the ridge of the roof.

The best answer is a combination of air inlets in the eaves plus a thermostatically controlled power vent mounted in the roof near the ridge. The power vent runs on electricity, but it will save far more than it uses.

Your attic needs 10 changes of air per hour. To ventilate the entire attic area, you can calculate the power vent capacity you need from the accompanying chart prepared by the Home Ventilating Institute. Find the length of your attic in the vertical column at the left of the chart, the width in the horizontal column along the top, and the capacity you need where the two columns intersect.

But if you have walled off a living area that you can vent with windows, subtract the cubic feet of this new room. Do this by multiplying the length times the width times the height. This might leave you with two smaller areas that need ventilating.

That diminishes the problem, but it doesn't eliminate it. The cheapest solution is to install louvered vents at each end for cross-ventilation, plus continuous screened vents in the soffits.

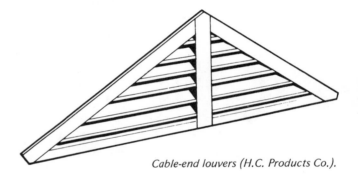

Cable-end louvers (H.C. Products Co.).

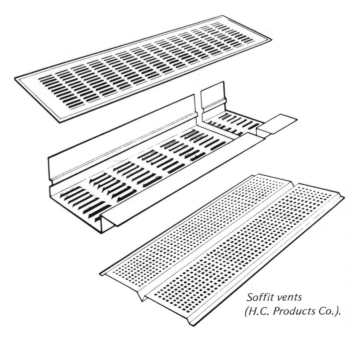

Soffit vents (H.C. Products Co.).

NET FREE AREA (SQ. IN.) TO VENTILATE ATTIC

Length (in feet)	Width (in feet) 20	22	24	26	28	30	32	34	36	38	40	42	44	46	48	50
20	192	211	230	250	269	288	307	326	346	365	384	403	422	441	461	480
22	211	232	253	275	296	317	338	359	380	401	422	444	465	485	506	528
24	230	253	276	300	323	346	369	392	415	438	461	484	507	530	553	576
26	250	275	300	324	349	374	399	424	449	474	499	524	549	574	599	624
28	269	296	323	349	376	403	430	457	484	511	538	564	591	618	645	662
30	288	317	346	374	403	432	461	490	518	547	576	605	634	662	691	720
32	307	338	369	399	430	461	492	522	553	584	614	645	675	706	737	768
34	326	359	392	424	457	490	522	555	588	620	653	685	717	750	782	815
36	346	380	415	449	484	518	553	588	622	657	691	726	760	795	829	864
38	365	401	438	474	511	547	584	620	657	693	730	766	803	839	876	912
40	384	422	461	499	538	576	614	653	691	730	768	806	845	883	922	960
42	403	444	484	524	564	605	645	685	726	766	806	847	887	927	968	1008
44	422	465	507	549	591	634	676	718	760	803	845	887	929	971	1013	1056
46	442	486	530	574	618	662	707	751	795	839	883	927	972	1016	1060	1104
48	461	507	553	599	645	691	737	783	829	876	922	968	1014	1060	1106	1152
50	480	528	576	624	672	720	768	816	864	912	960	1008	1056	1104	1152	1200
52	499	549	599	649	699	749	799	848	898	948	998	1048	1098	1148	1198	1248
54	518	570	622	674	726	778	830	881	933	985	1037	1089	1141	1192	1244	1296
56	538	591	645	699	753	807	860	914	967	1021	1075	1130	1184	1237	1291	1345
58	557	612	668	724	780	835	891	946	1002	1058	1113	1170	1226	1282	1337	1392
60	576	634	691	749	807	864	922	979	1037	1094	1152	1210	1267	1324	1382	1440
62	595	655	714	774	834	893	953	1012	1071	1131	1190	1250	1309	1369	1428	1488
64	614	676	737	799	861	922	983	1045	1106	1168	1229	1291	1352	1413	1475	1536
66	634	697	760	824	888	950	1014	1077	1140	1204	1268	1331	1394	1458	1522	1585
68	653	718	783	849	914	979	1045	1110	1175	1240	1306	1371	1436	1501	1567	1632
70	672	739	806	874	941	1008	1075	1142	1210	1276	1344	1411	1478	1545	1613	1680

FHA Chart Chart utilizes 1/300 ratio; double for 1/150 ratio; divide by five for 1/1500 ratio.

Chart gives the amount of net free area (in square inches) required to ventilate attic space of home. To use chart, measure length and width of each rectangular section of your attic. Locate length dimensions on the vertical column and width dimensions on the horizontal column.

POWER VENTILATOR REQUIREMENTS

LENGTH IN FEET	WIDTH IN FEET 20	22	24	26	28	30	32	34	36	38	40	42	44	46	48	50
20	280	308	336	364	392	420	448	476	504	532	560	588	616	644	672	700
22	308	339	370	400	431	462	493	524	554	585	616	647	678	708	739	770
24	336	370	403	437	470	504	538	571	605	638	672	706	739	773	806	840
26	364	400	437	473	510	546	582	619	655	692	728	764	801	837	874	910
28	392	431	470	510	549	588	627	666	706	745	784	823	862	902	941	980
30	420	462	504	546	588	630	672	714	756	798	840	882	924	966	1008	1050
32	448	493	538	582	627	672	717	761	806	851	896	941	986	1030	1075	1120
34	476	524	571	619	666	714	762	809	857	904	952	1000	1047	1095	1142	1190
36	504	554	604	655	706	756	806	857	907	958	1008	1058	1109	1159	1210	1260
38	532	585	638	692	745	798	851	904	958	1011	1064	1117	1170	1224	1277	1330
40	560	616	672	728	784	840	896	952	1008	1064	1120	1176	1232	1288	1344	1400
42	588	647	706	764	823	882	941	1000	1058	1117	1176	1234	1294	1352	1411	1470
44	616	678	739	801	862	924	986	1047	1109	1170	1232	1294	1355	1417	1478	1540
46	644	708	773	837	902	966	1030	1095	1159	1224	1288	1352	1417	1481	1546	1610
48	672	739	806	874	941	1008	1075	1142	1210	1277	1344	1411	1478	1546	1613	1680
50	700	770	840	910	980	1050	1120	1190	1260	1330	1400	1470	1540	1610	1680	1750
52	728	801	874	946	1019	1092	1165	1238	1310	1383	1456	1529	1602	1674	1747	1820
54	756	832	907	983	1058	1134	1210	1285	1361	1436	1512	1588	1663	1739	1814	1890
56	784	862	941	1019	1098	1176	1254	1333	1411	1490	1568	1646	1725	1803	1882	1960
58	812	893	974	1056	1137	1218	1299	1380	1462	1543	1624	1705	1786	1868	1949	2030
60	840	924	1008	1092	1176	1260	1344	1428	1512	1596	1680	1764	1848	1932	2016	2100
62	868	955	1042	1128	1215	1302	1389	1476	1562	1649	1736	1823	1910	1996	2083	2170
64	896	986	1075	1165	1254	1344	1434	1523	1613	1702	1792	1882	1971	2061	2150	2240
66	924	1016	1108	1201	1294	1386	1478	1571	1663	1756	1848	1940	2033	2125	2218	2310
68	952	1047	1142	1238	1333	1428	1523	1618	1714	1809	1904	1999	2094	2190	2285	2380
70	980	1078	1176	1274	1372	1470	1568	1666	1764	1862	1960	2058	2156	2254	2352	2450

HVI Chart

To determine what size power ventilator is needed to cool your attic efficiently, find the length of your attic on the vertical column and the width on the horizontal column. Where two columns intersect, you will find the required CFM rated ventilator (Courtesy of Home Ventilating Institute).

Combination of Masonite's woodgrain and Shale White paneling was used to make a multi-purpose bedroom in this attic, by Ethel Samuels, NSID. In this view of one end of the room she used the bedspread fabric to cover the odd shape of mini-dormer, put built-in storage under window for bed linens, and lighted window alcove with hidden fluorescent tube. At left is mother's work area.

At husband's end of room she used the woodgrain paneling, and built shelving for television and books. Window shade reflects pattern at other end of room.

Decor

When an attic is finished off it usually is a much more personal room than you could create in a basement. A basement is only one floor down from the main living area, so it can supplement it or complement it. It becomes an extension of the main living area.

But an attic is two flights of stairs removed from that first floor. It is too far away for a party or for a game room. Besides, it seldom offers very much space. You might finish it off as an extra bedroom, perhaps a guest room, perhaps a study. In any event, being more personal, there are different options for the finishing.

For example, you wouldn't use a quilted wallcovering in a basement party room — probably. But in an attic bedroom for a specific member of the family, this might be excellent. It could be a playroom that isolates the noise of play from the remainder of the house. It might be large enough to provide a suite or separate apartment for some member of the family who needs one.

However you decide to use it, it represents space you have paid for; it should not be wasted. Not only will it give you added room, but the finishing you do in even a small attic can make a big difference to a prospective purchaser, if ever you decide you want to sell the house.

A

Attic finished off with wallboard, painted, relies on fabrics and shades for decor. Basis here is Riverdale's "Petite Pizzazz" collection, used as window shades and as shades to pull down and hide storage areas at left. Porthole mirrors decorate wall, and three sofa beds are built up along far wall and at right. The fabric is ironed on to the walls, and to the laminated window shades. This is apartment of Designer Peg Walker.

More conventional, but very effective finishing of attic is this suggestion by American Plywood Assn. (A) with conventional window, or (B) with floor-to-rafter windows. Windows might have to be installed to get natural light. Roof pitch can simply be painted provided insulation was put in by the builder; or, add insulation between rafters and then install plywood panel rafters, then paint. Both of these attics are finished off to provide storage, primarily, although B provides an area for amateur painter. Note also the hanging plywood shelves in B for storage.

B

Waverly Fabrics' "Wood Violets" is used here on walls as well as in soft applications to create a girl's room in an attic dormer. Don't overlook possibilities of fabrics in finishing off attics.

This attic was finished off as a general living area, with a built-in cooktop at right, eating area at windows. Wall-Tex fabric-backed wallcovering was used on window shades, walls, other areas.

Although what you do with your attic space will depend on its conformation and your personal taste and desire, there are a few points worth mentioning.

First, while your house is still a shell, be sure you bring the heating-cooling duct up to the attic space before you close off the lower levels. You can buy a sheet metal extension for this purpose at your home center.

Wiring

When adding more load to the electrical system, such as added wiring for a room in the attic, be sure to check the electrical service first so as not to overload. Shown is a typical layout of the various circuits. You can add an entire new circuit by adding a new circuit-breaker and running the line up to the attic.

In running wire, drill holes in studs to run it to wall boxes which will be in the wall everywhere you will want a switch or outlet.

You will be using #12 two-conductor cable in most cases, #12 three-conductor cable where you will have three-way switches. Run cable along a running board if you do not drill holes (see lower diagram). Staple it every 4-1/2 feet, but always within 12 inches of a wall box.

See wiring diagrams on facing page for ways to extend existing wiring to new wall boxes.

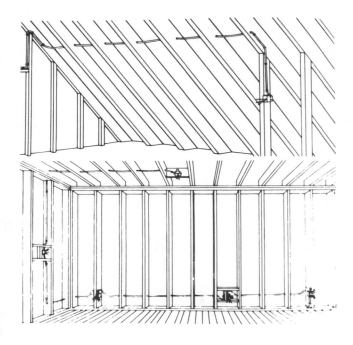

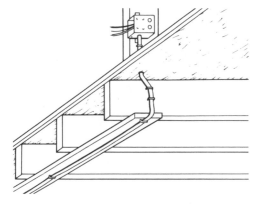

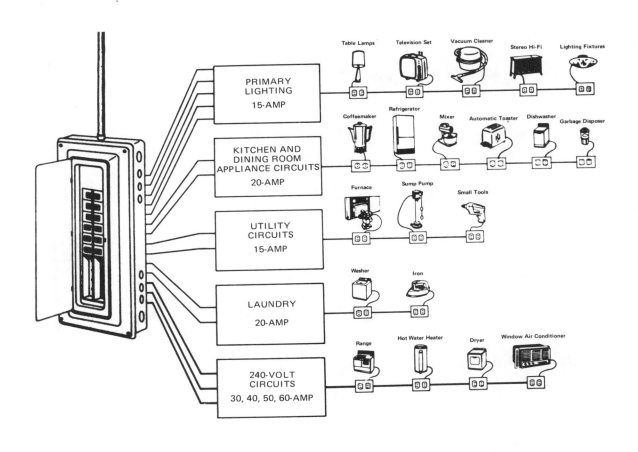

PRIMARY
LIGHTING
15-AMP

Table Lamps · Television Set · Vacuum Cleaner · Stereo Hi-Fi · Lighting Fixtures

KITCHEN AND
DINING ROOM
APPLIANCE CIRCUITS
20-AMP

Coffeemaker · Refrigerator · Mixer · Automatic Toaster · Dishwasher · Garbage Disposer

UTILITY
CIRCUITS
15-AMP

Furnace · Sump Pump · Small Tools

LAUNDRY
20-AMP

Washer · Iron

240-VOLT
CIRCUITS
30, 40, 50, 60-AMP

Range · Hot Water Heater · Dryer · Window Air Conditioner

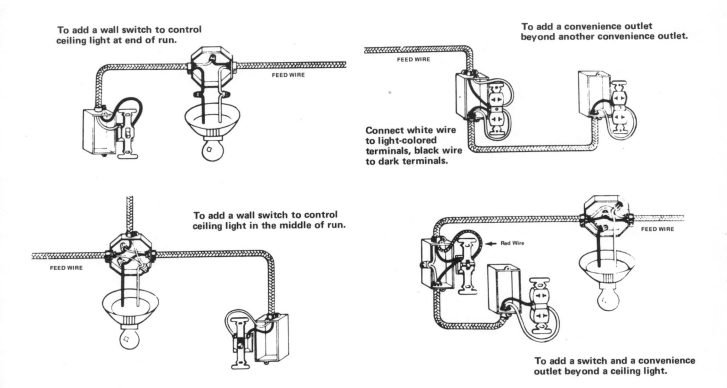

To add a wall switch to control ceiling light at end of run.

FEED WIRE

To add a wall switch to control ceiling light in the middle of run.

FEED WIRE

To add a convenience outlet beyond another convenience outlet.

FEED WIRE

Connect white wire to light-colored terminals, black wire to dark terminals.

← Red Wire

FEED WIRE

To add a switch and a convenience outlet beyond a ceiling light.

Raise the Roof for Dormer or Skylights

Attic space always is small for an obvious reason: the roof slopes. If you are willing to raise one sloping side of the roof you can create a shed-type dormer and a room that runs the entire length of the house.

Then you can put some real magic into it by adding a skylight, or two, or three.

If you want to do this, first check the floor of the attic. Throughout the house, builders have put studs and joists 16 inches on center. But the attic floor often has joists 24 inches on center because the assumption is that few people will be walking around up there. You'll have to fill in the floor of your new room with extra joists that are the same size as the joists already there, and toe-nail them in so they are solid and will support whatever weight you will put into your new room.

The drawing on p. 99 shows the general construction details of the roof and an added dormer. The dormer drawing assumes a roof high enough to have a separate ceiling, but in many cases you will simply finish off the underside of the roof, insulate it and sheath it so it can serve as the ceiling.

Beyond this, note that building a dormer involves a structural change in the house. You will need a building permit. And while it looks simple, it is complicated. The safest way is to contract the job out. Let a contractor do at least the structural part of it. You can then replace the roofing material and do all the interior finishing.

If you want the special magic of skylights, you can install them yourself in the new dormer roof — or any other part of the roof. A fact few people realize is that you can install a skylight even in an unfinished attic, for the room below the attic. The way to do this is to install the skylight in the roof, then construct a simple plywood "light shaft" through the attic crawl space to the room below (see drawings).

There are several brands and types of skylights, including some that can be opened for ventilation. The instructions here showing installation procedure apply to other types, but these are by Skymaster, for the plastic "bubble" type. Note one version is "curb-mounted," which raises it slightly above roof level, and the other fits cleanly into the roofing shingles.

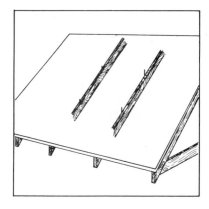

1. *Allow yourself 2 to 4 hours of clear weather for the job. To install Skymaster low-profile skylight, which fits cleanly in with shingles and has no curb, drive 3-in. nail up through the roof at the four corners marking the location of your skylight. Be sure there are no electrical wires, pipes or ducts in the way.*

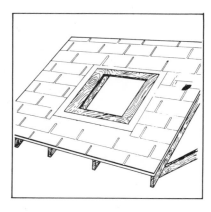

2. *Go up on the roof, locate the nails protruding through, and remove roofing material back about 12 in. around the area. Cut hole through the roof decking.*

3. *Frame the opening, top and bottom. Rafters will form the sides of the framing. If you are using a bigger skylight and rafter runs through the opening, cut the rafter back to make room for the new framing.*

4. Apply roofing mastic around the opening about 1/4 in. thick, covering all exposed wood and felt. Use a black roofing mastic such as GAF, Johns-Manville, Bird & Son, or similar.

7. Apply mastic over the felt strips and replace shingles. After shingles are in place, apply mastic across the bottom of the skylight, as shown in small drawing at lower left.

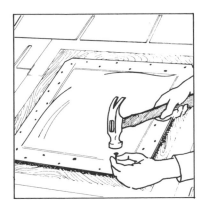

5. Position skylight over the opening. Drill small holes for the nails. Nail each corner down in line with the rafter, with a 6d or 8d nail. Use 3/4-in. rustproof roofing nails around the flange, about 3 in. apart.

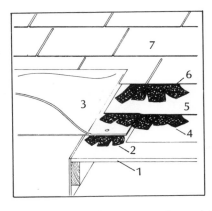

8. This drawing shows the sequence of materials: 1, roof deck; 2, mastic; 3, skylight; 4, mastic; 5, roofing felt; 6, mastic; 7, shingles.

6. Apply mastic over the edge of skylight right up to the bubble. Cut strips of roofing felt wide enough to go from the bubble to overlap the felt on the deck. Apply more mastic over these strips at the top and apply the top strip of felt. Don't put a strip on the bottom.

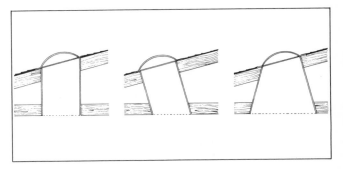

9. If you want to make a light shaft you can angle it to direct the sunlight. Straight down is best, but if there is some obstruction you can avoid it by angling the shaft. You also might want to make the bottom of the shaft bigger to distribute the light over a broader area. You can use 1/4-in. plywood or hardboard for the shaft, paint the inside white, leave the bottom open or cut a plastic diffuser to cover it.

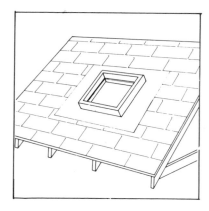

5. For a curb-type skylight, steps 1 through 4 are the same as for low-profile model. (See preceding pages). Then construct the curb with 2x6 lumber. This will go on top of the roof deck, so inside dimensions of curb will be same as the opening. Be sure to use mastic in all joints.

8. Replace shingles.

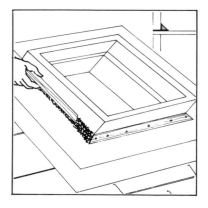

6. Apply mastic on the outside of the curb at the bottom, and nail cant strips in place. These are triangular moldings that will hold the curb in place.

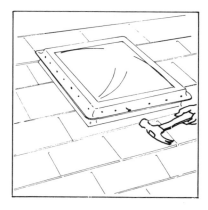

9. Apply a bead of clear mastic around the top edge of the curb and press skylight down into place. Drill small holes for nails or screws and secure flange around edge about every 3 in.

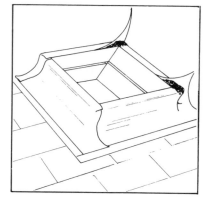

7. Cover entire outside of curb with mastic, then cover with strips of roofing felt. First put on the bottom one, then the sides, then the top. Be sure to apply mastic everywhere the felt overlaps, and cover all exposed seams with mastic.

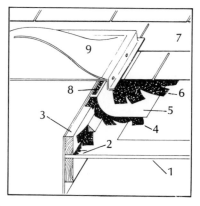

10. Sequence here is: 1, roof deck; 2, mastic; 3, curb; 4, mastic; 5, roofing felt; 6, mastic; 7, shingles; 8, clear mastic; 9, skylight.

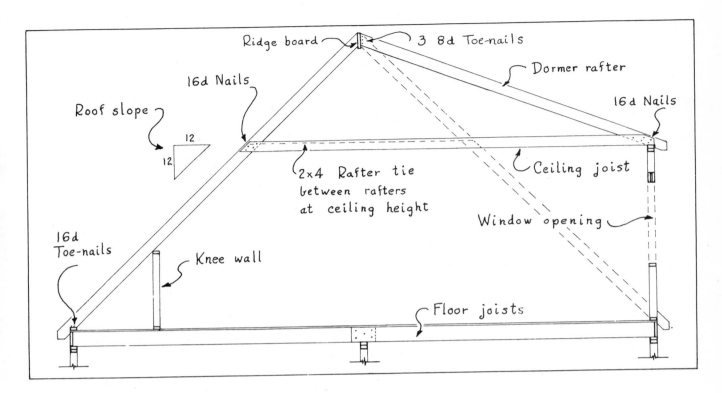

This cross-section of story-and-a-half framing shows how a shed-style dormer can extend usable floor space and the full height of a ceiling on an attic room. Such dormers are normally used only on the home's rear. Dotted lines indicate original roof line. (Reproduced from How to Build Your Own Home, a Successful Book by Robert C. Reschke).

10. Kitchens: Pick your best options

If your builder will do the electrical and plumbing rough-in in your kitchen, but otherwise leave it bare, you can save a bundle on the purchase price of the home.

But wait. Think it over carefully, and consult with him.

Options

The builder can buy cabinets and appliances at half the price you will pay; he usually buys on a lowest-bid basis, and you will buy at retail. But his standard products generally will be of lower quality than you would buy for yourself.

Your options with a cooperative builder fall into the following categories.

Entirely Bare

Have the builder leave the kitchen entirely bare. For this he probably will knock off about $1,000 from the house price. You, however, will probably pay at least $2,000 for cabinets, countertops, sink, faucet, refrigerator, range, dishwasher and disposer, ceiling light fixture and coverings for floor, ceiling and walls. This would be minimal, and you could easily spend $4,000, or even $8,000, for what you really want in your kitchen.

Builder-Supplied Appliances

Buy your appliances, cabinets and tops from the builder, but uninstalled. Follow his design to install everything yourself. This would save you up to $500 on the purchase price of the house and it would be the cheapest way for you to buy your basic kitchen equipment.

Upgraded Products

Buy your appliances uninstalled from the builder, but ask him for upgraded products — better cabinets, a self-cleaning oven, a frostfree refrigerator. This would wipe out any savings, but you would end up with a finer kitchen and you would probably be a lot happier with it.

"Starter" Kitchen Kits

Have him leave it bare, design your own kitchen, then buy a promotional "starter" kitchen at a home center that will include sink and faucet, sink front, five wall cabinets, and two base cabinets. You can add a range and refrigerator (plain vanilla), and come out at about the same figure you saved on the price of the house. The only advantage to this is that you have an expandable design of your own, can add to it later, and come out with a better kitchen, possibly, than the builder would have provided. The disadvantage is that you will end up with cheap products. You can improve this option by buying better products that will add at least $600 to your costs.

The Cost Factor

In deciding among your options, costs will be a main consideration. If buying a new house, rather than updating your present one, be sure you get an accurate and complete list of all closing costs and move-in costs, so you will know how much money you have available or must borrow. Then decide whether it is worth it to pay the high interest of a short-term loan for your kitchen equipment.

Family Needs

Check the kitchen provided by the builder — look in the model home or on the floorplan. Check it for storage space in the cabinets, for countertop space, for functional efficiency and traffic flow. You may find there are too few cabinets or not enough counter space, or you may find it adequate. Either way, it will affect your options. Builders and their architects must design by averages, for average needs of average families. Your family might do a lot more cooking and need more pan and dish storage. You might entertain a lot and need much more glassware storage. If you're big on baking, it requires more counter space than the average. Think it through. Later in this chapter we'll show you how to solve these problems without stretching the walls.

Having said all that, we should point out that there are some builders who will make it remarkably easy for you. For example, Ridge Homes, to name one company that is available nationwide, offers all of the many kitchen cabinet styles made by Riviera — both are owned by Evans Products Co. Ridge offers all interior materials precision-cut to fit, with manuals telling you how to do it, and with upgrade options on appliances and kitchen design, all available to you at the builder price.

But builders differ and you may have other preferences. So we will go into detail.

These are the Steps You'll go Through

The steps from bare walls to your completed kitchen are:

1. Design it.

2. Sketch simple elevations and a floorplan to help you visualize, check measurements, and make an equipment list.

3. Plan your installation, writing down what you are going to do, in sequence. Check with your local government here on what must be inspected, and when.

4. Buy the equipment, and get it in the house before you start. Check it carefully for sizes ordered, color match, shipping damage, but keep it boxed for protection until each item is ready to install.

5. Prepare the room for installation, and install.

Design Starts with Planning for Your Needs

Kitchen design is not simply a matter of filling space with cabinets and appliances. It starts with the kind of family you have.

How big is the family, or how big do you plan it to be? More people mean more cabinet storage and counter area. Do you entertain a lot? You might want a bar area. Does the man like to barbecue? You might want a separate grill area away from the normal work area, possibly combined with a bar and bar sink. Do you want a display area for fine dishes or crystal? Do you want plants? Do you want a breakfast-lunch bar?

So first make a list of all the things you want in your kitchen, and involve everyone in the family in making the list.

Then make a list of your storage needs. There are generally six categories of things to be stored in the kitchen, and you will want to estimate your needs for each category.

Foods. These will include perishables such as meats and vegetables which will store in the refrigerator, so how big a refrigerator will you need? If you like to buy bulk meats you might want a separate freezer in a utility room or basement, and that would mean you won't need a two-door refrigerator with separate freezer. Think; you are planning for years ahead, too. Then there are canned and packaged foods and you will want to store at least a one-week supply. There will be breads and pastries, and such items as potatoes and onions. All must have a place.

Utensils, small appliances. This will include flatware, which will go in a drawer; utility items, such as a spatula, tongs, etc.; pots and pans; toaster, waffle iron, mixer, blender, other such items (which you should list because everything will need a place); and, a dishpan or drying rack if you don't plan a dishwasher.

Dishes. This will include china, glassware, silverware, utility dishes. Here you might plan other places for things such as fine china or silverware, such as a cabinet in the dining room.

Soft goods. This would include kitchen linen, paper towels, place mats, napkins, foil, etc.

Cleaning supplies. This includes soaps and detergents, brooms, mops, pails.

Trash. Will you want a trash compactor?

Now you have a good idea of what you must store. The next question is: where? And the answer, which will help save thousands of steps over the years, is to store each thing at the point of first or last use. That means, for example, that breakfast dishes should be stored either at the breakfast bar (first use) or near the sink where they are cleaned (last use). But dinner dishes would be stored near the dining room or near the sink.

So now start thinking of the areas you will have in your kitchen. There will be a sink and clean-up area, and of course that's where you will want to store many of your cleaning materials. There will be a food preparation and mixing area, where you will want to store many utensils and have many small appliances handy, plus utility dishes. There will be a refrigeration and storage area, a range and cooking area, and a serving area.

The Shapes of Kitchens; The Work Triangle

You will arrange these work areas into a kitchen. Its simplest form would be on one wall, which might be necessary because of space limitations. Almost as simple is the two-wall, or "corridor" kitchen, but this is not a desirable plan because it leaves no room for other activities, such as a breakfast area, and traffic can interfere. The L-shaped kitchen would, as the name indicates, have all kitchen equipment arranged on two adjacent walls, and this is usually the most workable and efficient, and the most

U-Shaped Kitchen   **L-Shaped Kitchen**   **Corridor Kitchen**   **One-Wall Kitchen**

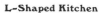
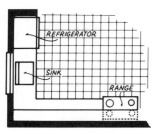

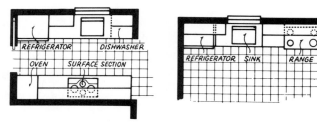

common. But where space permits you will want a U-shaped kitchen, as it affords the most efficient work patterns with ample space but not too many steps between areas.

As you consider the various possible layouts, make rough sketches of them and then draw lines connecting the center of the sink, the center of the refrigerator and the center of the range. These connected lines comprise what kitchen planners call the "work triangle." For efficiency and step-saving, the total distance along the work triangle should not be more than 22 feet and not less than 12 feet. And no single leg of that triangle should be more than 9 feet, or less than 4 feet.

Basic Kitchen Measurements

Now let's consider some of the basic measurements.

Overall height, from the floor to the top of your wall cabinets, will be 84 inches. Base cabinets are 34-1/2 inches high, which includes the kick space at the bottom. The slab of the countertop is 1-1/2 inches high. Wall cabinets are either 30 or 33 inches high, unless you get special sizes, and this gives you a "backsplash" area of 15 or 18 inches

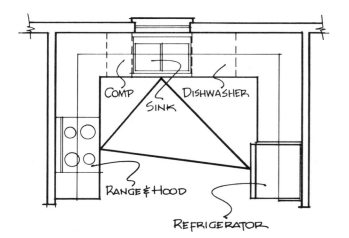

between the countertop and the bottom of the wall cabinets. This totals 84 inches, which means the top of your kitchen will square off with door and window framing. The area above the wall cabinets might be left open, or you might fill it in with what is called (universally, but erroneously) a soffit.

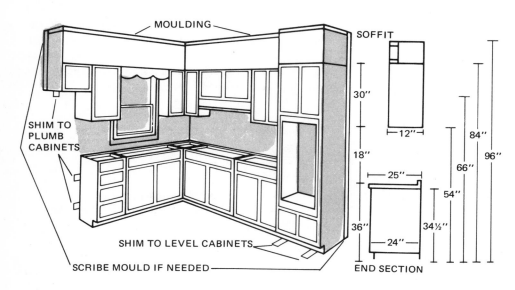

Drawing courtesy of Riviera Cabinets.

Base cabinets are 24 inches deep. Wall cabinets are 12 to 13 inches deep, varying slightly among manufacturers. Both base and wall cabinets are made in 3-inch increments ranging down to 9 inches wide and up to 60 inches wide. Some wall cabinets are as little as 12 inches high, ranging up to 42 inches high by some manufacturers. But normally you will have to go to a custom kitchen dealer or local cabinet maker to get wall cabinets more than 30 inches high.

The bottoms of wall cabinets over the sink or the range should be higher, 60 inches from the floor. This allows for head room and working room over the sink, fire and heat protection over the range.

Your cabinets can be all wood, or wood with plastic laminate surfaces, or steel. There is only one custom manufacturer of steel kitchen cabinets in the U.S. — St. Charles — which also offers options of wood or plastic laminate drawer fronts and doors, or an all-wood and plastic laminate cabinet. There are many manufacturers of both wood and plastic laminate cabinets, and you will find a wide price range.

Appliances You Will Need

Ranges and refrigerators come in many sizes. The most common range size is 30 inches wide. Your refrigerator size will be determined by how much capacity you need. Built-in dishwashers are 24 inches wide.

Trash compactors are usually 15 inches wide, although Waste King makes a space saver at 12 inches wide.

Kitchen sinks come in various sizes and conformations with one, two or three bowls.

With no dishwasher, you will want at least two bowls for handling dishes. The third bowl in a 3-bowl model is usually a small one for such functions as mixing salads or cleaning vegetables, and many designers like to put the disposer in the third bowl.

Dishwashers are becoming almost a standard item in kitchens today. An automatic dishwasher uses from 10 to 12 gallons of water for normal cycles — often less water than washing the dishes by hand. And dishwashers give thorough, bacteria-free results.

There are five types of fully automatic dishwashers; each has its own advantages.

Built-in. These undercounter types are permanently connected to water lines, drain pipe, and electric circuits. They are incorporated into the surrounding kitchen cabinets, which muffles the sound. And frequently the front panel of the dishwasher can be the same material as that used for the cabinets.

Free-Standing. Similar to built-in undercounter models, the free-standing unit is designed to take up otherwise unused area or to sit at the end of a counter. Units come with porcelain surround as well as with decorative panels of plastic laminate or hardwood.

Convertible. These are automatic dishwashers with front-end loading that are installed initially on casters with the recognition that later the unit will be taken to a new home and installed as part of the cabinetry, either as an undercounter unit or a free-standing model.

Portable. Requirements include a wall outlet for plugging in and a hose which connects to the spout of your kitchen faucet. This unit can be rolled to the table for filling and later moved to another room, if desired, for storage. Portables can be obtained for top loading, or front-end loading on "convertible" models that may later be built into the kitchen.

Dishwasher-Sink. This compact unit combines sink top, bowl, cabinet, faucets, and dishwasher. They are usually metal.

Requirements for installing a dishwasher include a water supply that will flow at least 2 to 2.5 gallons per minute at a pressure of at least 15 pounds per square inch at a temperature of at least 140 degrees. Soft water is desirable but not necessary.

Your sink might be porcelain-on-steel (the lowest-priced), or stainless steel or cast iron. Or you might choose a DuPont Corian countertop with an integral bowl molded right in, an expensive option. Corian is a man-made marble that is workable with ordinary tools.

You will want a ducted ventilating hood over your range. Don't try to cut corners to eliminate this appliance, because it means cleaner air in the house, fewer odors, cleaner curtains and draperies, cleaner shelves. The ductwork should take the shortest path to the nearest outside wall. By paying a little more you can get a quieter squirrel-cage blower rather than a conventional fan in the hood, and this is important because a fan can be very noisy. The bottom of your hood should be 24 inches above the cooking surface, and for this distance you will want at least a 200 cfm blower or fan, preferably a 300 cfm. (The blower's air movement is measured in cubic feet per minute, cfm, and any hood you buy should have a Home Ventilating Institute label with the cfm rating.)

A lower-priced option would be a ductless hood. This is not vented to the outside, and a fan recirculates the cooking air through filters and back into the kitchen. It helps on grease and odor, but its performance does not compare with a vented hood. The third and even cheaper option would be to locate the range near a window or outside wall, and installing an exhaust fan in the wall or in the window. But again, this is not a place to compromise; the vented hood is best.

Your Cabinets — Drawers or Shelves

Now let's consider the kinds of cabinets you will want. For general storage you will want the standard base cabinet that has one drawer at the top. How many of these will you need?

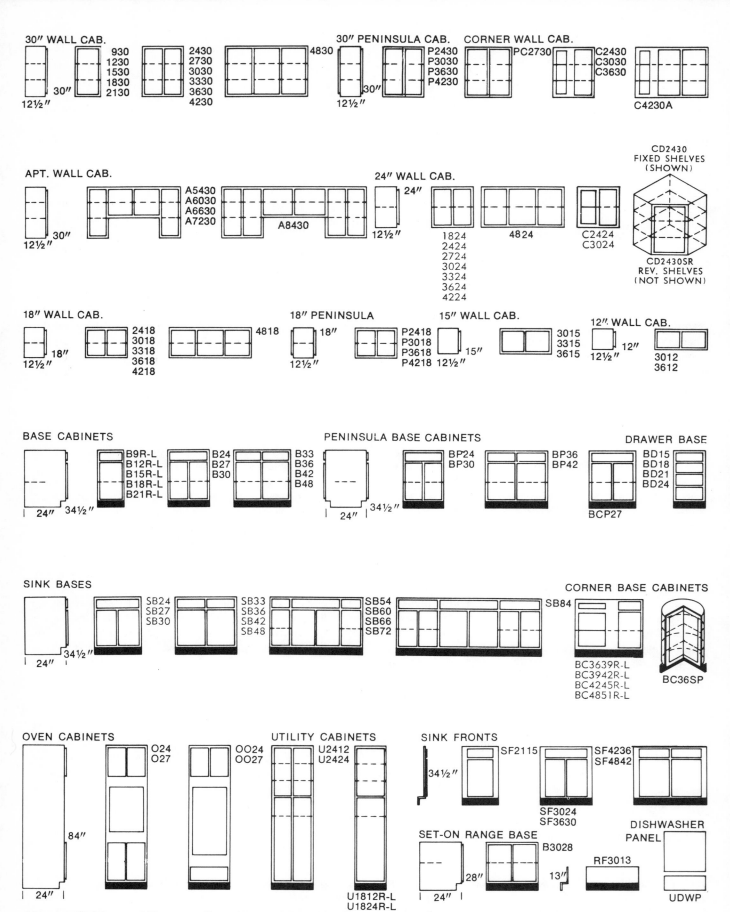

30″ WALL CAB.
930
1230
1530
1830
2130

2430
2730
3030
3330
3630
4230

4830

30″ PENINSULA CAB.
P2430
P3030
P3630
P4230

CORNER WALL CAB.
PC2730

C2430
C3030
C3630

C4230A

CD2430
FIXED SHELVES
(SHOWN)

CD2430SR
REV. SHELVES
(NOT SHOWN)

APT. WALL CAB.
A5430
A6030
A6630
A7230

A8430

24″ WALL CAB.
1824
2424
2724
3024
3324
3624
4224

4824

C2424
C3024

18″ WALL CAB.
2418
3018
3318
3618
4218

4818

18″ PENINSULA
P2418
P3018
P3618
P4218

15″ WALL CAB.
3015
3315
3615

12″ WALL CAB.
3012
3612

BASE CABINETS
B9R-L
B12R-L
B15R-L
B18R-L
B21R-L

B24
B27
B30

B33
B36
B42
B48

PENINSULA BASE CABINETS
BP24
BP30

BP36
BP42

BCP27

DRAWER BASE
BD15
BD18
BD21
BD24

SINK BASES
SB24
SB27
SB30

SB33
SB36
SB42
SB48

SB54
SB60
SB66
SB72

SB84

CORNER BASE CABINETS
BC3639R-L
BC3942R-L
BC4245R-L
BC4851R-L

BC36SP

OVEN CABINETS
O24
O27

OO24
OO27

UTILITY CABINETS
U2412
U2424

U1812R-L
U1824R-L

SINK FRONTS
SF2115

SF4236
SF4842

SF3024
SF3630

SET-ON RANGE BASE
B3028

RF3013

DISHWASHER PANEL

UDWP

Also available: moldings, wall and base fillers, paneling, accessories, hardware options.

Drawing courtesy of Westinghouse Co.

For pot and pan storage you also will want this standard one-drawer cabinet. How many for this purpose?

For dry vegetable storage and for breads and cakes, the most practical is a three-drawer base cabinet. This has no shelves, just drawers. How many of these?

For the sink you will need either a sink front (cheapest, because it is not a cabinet, just a front that hides the under-sink area and connects to the cabinets on either side.), or a sink cabinet, which is better because it gives you a cabinet floor for storage of your cleaning materials. It also is practical to plan a two-drawer base cabinet (two drawers and one shelf) in the sink area.

For your food preparation area you will want a base cabinet with pull-out shelves for your mixer, small appliances and similar items. This can be with one drawer or no drawer.

There are special cabinets for built-in wall ovens, tall cabinets for brooms or pantry use ranging from 12 to 42 inches wide and 12 to 24 inches deep and 84 inches high, and there are many other specials available from custom kitchen dealers. Pantry cabinets might have built-in

shelving, or Lazy Susan shelves, or hinged shelving systems that fold out for maximum use of space. They often have condiment shelves on the inside of the door, and can solve a lot of storage problems.

Now You are Ready to Start Designing

By now you have probably visited kitchen showrooms or studied equipment lists available from your builder. You know what sink you want, and its measurements; the appliances and their measurements; the types of cabinets and their sizes. You know everything you want, and now you will plan where to put everything.

Measure the room accurately. Measure the entire room, not just the parts you think you will need, because it helps your accuracy. Don't rely on the builder's floorplan without checking the measurements, because floorplans often can be off by inches and that could blow your design. Include all measurements of windows and doors, and their framings.

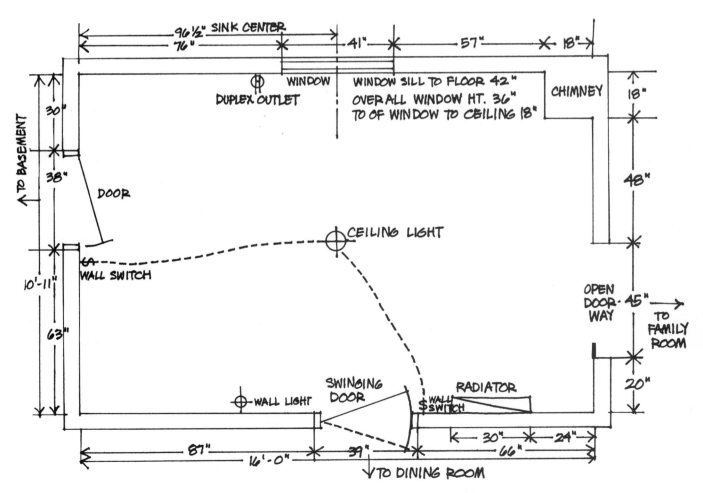

Example of a scale drawing of an existing kitchen showing basic measurements — no cabinets or appliances. This is how your drawing should look before you start positioning your new appliances and cabinets.

Put all this on graph paper marked off in half-inch increments. Your plan will be on a half-inch scale, with each half-inch increment on your graph paper representing one foot in the kitchen. Mark the electrical lead-ins and the plumbing rough-in.

Stop and think now. Will you want more electrical outlets? Sooner or later you will want at least three double outlets over your main work counter. You may have to add wiring for a disposer or a dishwasher. Even if these will be delayed purchases, now is the best time to do the electrical rough-in while the kitchen is still totally bare. And will you want an ice-maker in the refrigerator, now or later? If so, you will have to run a quarter-inch line of copper tubing (or other water supply) from the nearest cold-water supply pipe to where it can supply your ice-maker.

Sketch these onto your graph paper with dotted lines. They are things you must do before you start installation.

Cabinets and Appliances

Now for the designing. It normally starts with the window, if there is one. But in this case your builder already has roughed in the plumbing, so you will start with the sink.

Draw it in where the plumbing is roughed in. Then draw in your dishwasher adjacent to the sink, either left or right, depending on which way you like to work. If you are not planning to buy a dishwasher now, put a 24-inch base cabinet there. At some later date you can simply pull the cabinet and replace it with the dishwasher. Don't delude yourself. You will want a dishwasher sooner or later.

Then continue around the wall, drawing in each base cabinet and marking it for size and type ("24" 1-drawer, "21" 3-drawer, etc.) and, if necessary, adjust these sizes so the run of cabinets ends up where you want it to end up. And don't kid yourself. If you design-in 135 inches of cabinets, they are *not* going to fit into 134-3/4 inches of space. They are not going to fit into 135 inches, either, if there is a wall at both ends. Allow an inch on a run that long. Some cabinets have extended stiles (the vertical member of the face frame) that can be cut down to fit the wall. In other cases there are fillers for the extra inch.

Incidentally, when you measure the distance between walls at either end, measure along the baseboard and measure again 24 inches out from the wall. New walls are not necessarily straight and square, and you might find it's 135 inches along the wall and 136 inches out where the cabinet fronts will be.

In such a case, design your kitchen for the smallest dimension so you know it will fit. Here are some more figures to guide you in your design.

Your appliances need "landing space" on the counter-top — places to work and to put things down.

You need at least 24 inches, preferably 36 inches, to the right of the sink. You need at least 18 inches, preferably 30 inches, to the left of the sink. This is countertop space and is not necessarily affected by the cabinets beneath the countertop. But you must remember it in placing your range or cooktop.

A one-piece range needs at least 18 inches on each side, but it is best to have at least 24 inches on the inside of the work triangle. A built-in cooktop needs at least 18 inches on either side. A built-in oven needs 24 inches on the side you like to work on. There should be 18 inches of landing space on the door-opening side of the refrigerator. And, incidentally, be sure your refrigerator is hinged so the door opens for access from the inside of the work triangle. You don't want to be walking around the refrigerator door all the time. If your food preparation area is at your refrigerator, you need 36 to 42 inches of space here, rather than 18 inches.

If you are thinking as you go along, you will suddenly wonder: What do you do when you come to the inside corner of an L-shaped kitchen, or the two inside corners of a U?

Revolving shelf cabinet, commonly called "lazy susan," is one of best ways to turn an inside corner. This one is a pie-cut base cabinet, with shelves attached. Push it either way and it spins around.

Similar revolving shelf cabinet for wall installation makes corner space available. It is self-seating when it comes around to closed position.

You can't simply butt them, front edge to front edge. You would lose the space of the whole corner. And besides, it would leave no clearance for the knobs or pulls for the doors and drawers to open. A "base corner filler" can be used to separate them for clearance.

The best answer here is a corner cabinet with lazy susan shelves, giving you full access to all that space. This kind of cabinet takes 36 inches along each wall, but with lazy susan shelving this is all good storage space. A corner cabinet without lazy susan shelving gives you a lot of space you can't reach, because, remember, these base cabinets are 24 inches deep.

You also might buy diagonal corner cabinets. They look good, but they use a lot of wall space. For example, a diagonal corner cabinet that has a 20-inch diagonal door in front will take 39 inches on each wall. This doesn't waste space, but the space is hard to get to.

Manufacturers also offer a "blind base corner cabinet" which wastes about half of the space in the corner by extending into the corner. The last 12 inches or so of this cabinet, the part extending into the corner, has an unfinished surface against which you put the run of cabinets along the other wall, and with a small filler, usually three inches, to provide clearance for opening drawers and doors. The reach-in space is hard to use.

If the plumbing rough-in is near the corner you also can consider putting the sink in the corner diagonally, and

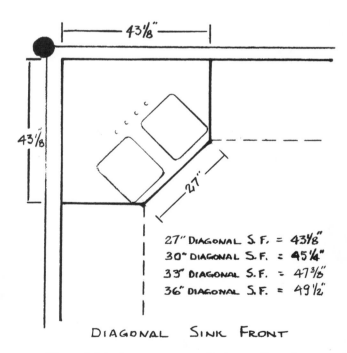

27" DIAGONAL S.F. = 43⅛"
30" DIAGONAL S.F. = 45¼"
33" DIAGONAL S.F. = 47⅜"
36" DIAGONAL S.F. = 49½"

DIAGONAL   SINK   FRONT

Diagonal sink placement, or use of other appliance in corner, is good way to turn when there is plenty of space in kitchen. This drawing shows how it uses wall space — 43-1/8 in. on each wall with a 27-in. front.

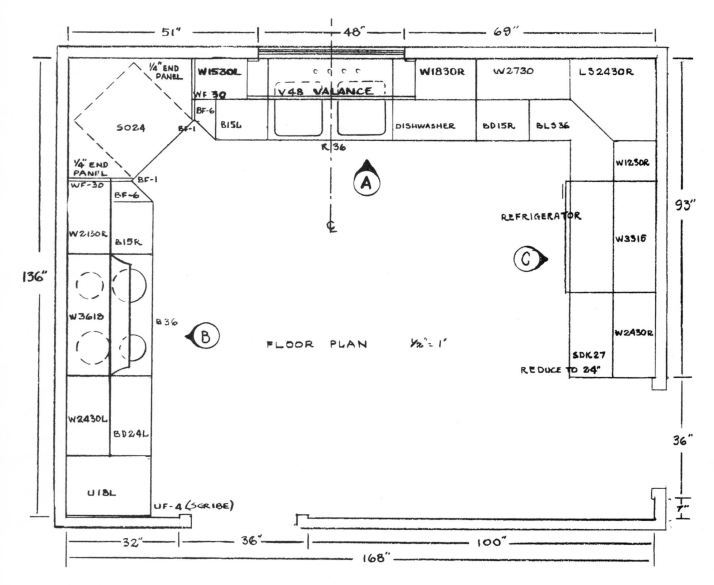

Typical floorplan gives sizes of all cabinets and appliances which you can check against your measurements. In coding of item numbers, "W" means wall cabinet, "B" means base cabinet, first two numbers in 4-number group are width, followed by height, and "R" or "L" following indicates on which side the door is hinged. Thus "W1830R" means a wall cabinet 18 in. wide, 30 in. deep, hinged right.

running a sink front across the corner. But for a 33-inch sink, your plumbing rough-in would have to be within 44 inches of the corner.

Your wall cabinets will correspond in widths with your base cabinets. They will be half as deep. So on your floorplan sketch, draw a dotted line 12 inches from the wall to indicate the wall cabinets where you want them.

This floorplan shows you your kitchen as it would look from above. You can check all of your measurements with it and draw in your work triangle to be sure it agrees with

the design principles already stated. You will want to note also that you have fillers to provide clearance in the corners and that you have at least 48 inches of working and walking space between cabinets or appliances on opposite walls.

And, as a final check, does the oven door open to block traffic at the door? Does the refrigerator door open to block entry or exit? Do these two doors open opposite each other to create an annoyance? Did you allow for the eating area you wanted?

Countertops

Then let's move on and consider your countertops.

The most common material for countertops is high-pressure plastic laminate, bonded to particleboard. Nationally known names are Formica, WilsonArt, Textolite, Micarta, Consoweld, Pionite, Melamite, Exxon Nevamar and, in the west, LaminArt.

You can buy the plastic surface and the particleboard substrate separately, and bond them yourself. But the bonding job must be perfect or it will delaminate, and it is better to be safe and buy an already-bonded "countertop blank" which will come in lengths up to 12 feet. You can cut it to size, and with a router you can cut the hole for the sink — carefully!

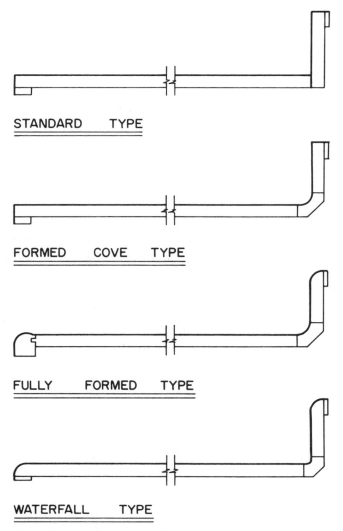

STANDARD TYPE

FORMED COVE TYPE

FULLY FORMED TYPE

WATERFALL TYPE

Cross-section of countertops, viewed from end, shows types. Standard type comes in two pieces with backsplash attached. Fromed types have no inside corner at back, making them easier to clean. Fully-formed type has "no-drip" edge.

If you buy the blank, it already will be built up to the proper 1-1/2-inch height, the front will be edged, and it will have its 5-inch backsplash. These are usually available at home centers, and you can get end caps which you will bond yourself at the end of the run.

If you are going to do it all yourself, buy 3/4-inch particleboard 25 inches deep and as long as you need. Specify industrial grade, not floor underlayment grade, and get a water-based contact adhesive for the bonding. Directions will be on the can. The plastic laminate itself comes in hundreds of colors and woodgrains, including metallics, slates and the popular butcher-block pattern. You will have to edge it, either with the same material or with a plastic or metal T-molding which hammers into place in a pre-cut groove. Some manufacturers now offer countertop kits with everything properly sized except for length, and except for the substrate. Be sure to get enough substrate to build it up along the perimeter to 1-1/2 inches.

Some people prefer ceramic tile for countertops, especially in the west and southwest. It can be beautiful, but tile must be grouted and this presents a cleaning problem that won't go away. (For instructions on how to tile a countertop, see Chapter 5.) Another expensive alternative is DuPont's Corian, a man-made marble that can be drilled, sawed and generally worked with woodworking tools and can be bought with the sink bowl molded in. It comes in 3/4-inch thickness, and must be built up to 1-1/2 inches around the perimeter. Flat sheets also come in 1/2-inch thickness, which lowers the price. It is a superb material, but look it over first to be sure you like it.

You have now settled on cabinets needed, their sizes, their placement, the appliance types and sizes and placement, and the kind of countertop You have sketched the whole kitchen in a floorplan.

Cabinet Style

Now you'll have to decide on cabinet style, for this sets the style of your entire kitchen. Do you want it in contemporary styling, with simple lines? Or traditional, or provincial, or early American, or what? Do you want your cabinets light or dark? Do you want the look of wood, or bright colors?

The best answer is to go look at the biggest kitchen displays in your area so you can see what's available. Your choices are practically limitless, and if you don't see what you like you simply haven't looked enough.

Look longer. Remember, you will live with this kitchen for many years and, unlike other rooms in the house, all elements will be permanently installed. Mistakes in other areas of the house can be relatively minor and inexpensive. In the kitchen any mistakes will be major and expensive. So be sure.

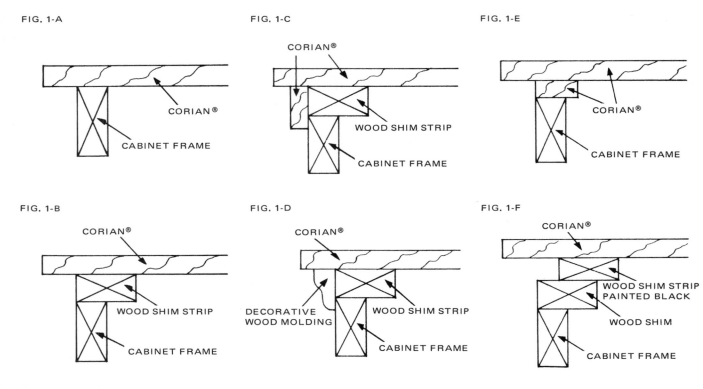

FIG. 1-A CORIAN® · CABINET FRAME

FIG. 1-C CORIAN® · WOOD SHIM STRIP · CABINET FRAME

FIG. 1-E CORIAN® · CABINET FRAME

FIG. 1-B CORIAN® · WOOD SHIM STRIP · CABINET FRAME

FIG. 1-D CORIAN® · DECORATIVE WOOD MOLDING · WOOD SHIM STRIP · CABINET FRAME

FIG. 1-F CORIAN® · WOOD SHIM STRIP PAINTED BLACK · WOOD SHIM · CABINET FRAME

Corian kitchen countertops come with or without integral sink bowl. Thickness of 3/4 in. is best, doubled around perimeter to bring top up to full 1-1/2 in. to match appliances, filling in center area with 3/4-in. particleboard filler. Sketches show edge treatments possible, from single sheet of Corian 3/4 or 1/2 in. thick in Fig. 1-A, with 3/4-in. particleboard shim strip added in 1-B, and other possibilities in 1-C through 1-F. Reason for the recessed shim in 1-F is to give illusion of a floating top.

Don't rely just on your home center for the cabinets, unless it has a complete kitchen department with several displays. Don't fail to inspect the displays of a custom kitchen dealer and note the construction of custom cabinets.

You may decide you want custom cabinets from a custom kitchen dealer. Most dealers will supply you with them on a cash-and-carry basis, although they prefer to install. But check it all out.

And don't overlook the possibility of having one of these custom kitchen dealers design your kitchen, even though you will install it yourself. If will cost you from $100 to $300, possibly more, but you will get professional design and you will get the right cabinets in the right places.

Now Plan Your Installation

Ask your builder if there are permits you must have, and who you must see to get them. In doing this you also will find out about necessary inspections required by your local building codes.

We suggested already that you have everything delivered before you start installing. Check on the delivery schedules on all equipment, particularly the cabinets. Make sure the cabinets are here and deliverable, not in some distant warehouse. If you are buying custom cabinets, they are not made until you order them; so it will take from 8 to 12 weeks for delivery. Make sure your appliances are in stock where you will buy them, and put a down payment on them to hold them.

Plan where you will put all this stuff after delivery and during installation, If you are buying a free-standing range, plan whether you can store it in the kitchen, along with the refrigerator, so you might use them before installation is completed. Things to be installed first should be nearest the kitchen. Make yourself a timetable for the entire job, and be sure to include in it the needed inspections. And in your planning, be sure to include the money you will need.

By now, to be realistic, we know you already have acquired many of the things that will go in your kitchen. Round it out and get everything into the house. Once you start the kitchen installation you will want to work straight through, and you won't want to keep walking out to the garage for each box. Get it in, open every box and check everything to be sure it is the right item, the right size, and undamaged.

The only exception here might be the countertop. Even good kitchen installers often leave the countertop until last — to eliminate error, and the high cost of error. After their base cabinets are in they measure again, and then buy the countertop.

Now You are Ready to Install

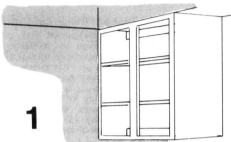

1 Starting in one corner, attach the corner wall cabinets to the wall using the 84" high "level line" or soffit as a guide for the top of the cabinet. Use screws through the hanging strips provided. Screws should be fastened to wall studs. Do not firmly tighten screws until all the cabinets are installed so final adjustments and necessary "shimming" can be done. Cabinets should always be attached to the walls with screws, **not** nails.

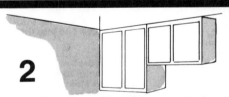

2 Following the cabinet layout, attach an adjoining cabinet to the wall. Make certain that the fronts (face frames) line up one to the other.

3 Using "C" clamps, pull the two adjoining cabinet face frame parts together and drill holes through the face frame of one cabinet, with one hole near the top, one near the bottom of the cabinets. Drill a "pilot" hole into the adjoining face frame.

4 Insert screws to tie the two cabinets together and draw up snug.

Cabinets

First, in all places where you will have wall cabinets, measure up 84 inches from the floor and draw a line on the wall. This line should locate precisely the tops of all your wall cabinets, and the tops of any tall cabinets such as a pantry or oven cabinet.

5 Continue with each adjoining wall cabinet in same way as in steps 2, 3 and 4.

6 Island Cabinets must be hung from the reinforcing strips w/screws, again remembering to *shim* where necessary.

7 After all wall cabinets have been hung in place, joined together, aligned and shimmed, the screws installed through the hanging strips into studs should be tightened securely to walls.

8 Base cabinets should be installed in a way similar to the way the wall cabinets were installed. Start with the corner base cabinets, mark stud locations, and predrill back rails for screws.

9 As each cabinet is installed, make certain that the fronts are plumb and straight, and level. Use shims to adjust units if necessary for uneven walls or floor. Lazy Susan Base should operate properly before attaching adjoining cabinets.

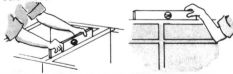

10 After all base cabinets have been installed in place, joined together, aligned and shimmed, the toe kick should be installed. Measure, cut and fit toe kick in place. Nail toe kick to cabinets with finish nails.

Several cabinet manufacturers have printed instructions to help you install cabinets. These instructions are from Riviera.

Make a similar line 34-1/2 inches above the floor in all areas where you will have base cabinets. Be sure to check first for high spots in the floor. Your line should be measured up from the highest point in the floor where cabinets will be installed. You may first have to draw a straight line along the floor, if the floor is uneven. You will have to shim up the low spots or the cabinets will not be level and the doors will rack.

Now check the wall surface in all areas that will be covered by cabinets. The walls must be smooth, level and true. Any high spots will have to be filed down, or low spots will require shims behind the cabinets, or the doors will rack.

Now you have a choice of starting with the wall cabinets or the base cabinets. If you start with the wall cabinets you eliminate the danger of bumping them against the base cabinets or dropping them on the bases, which would damage both. But if you do the base cabinets first, it is easier to hang the wall cabinets.

Let's do it the harder and safer way, starting with the wall cabinets. They will have to be screwed into the studs — not nailed — so locate and mark the centers of the studs. Make these marks above and below where the wall cabinets will fit, for easy visibility.

Make yourself a T-brace to hold the cabinet in place while you screw it to the wall. This might be a 2x3 or 2x4, a little longer than the distance from the floor to the bottom of the wall cabinet, with a 12-inch 2x2 nailed to the top to form a T. Fit a piece of carpet to the top and glue it on, to protect the cabinet it will support. Its overall length should be a few inches more than 54 inches, as these cabinets will be exactly 54 inches above the floor when in place and you will want to shift them up and down as you work.

Now start with the corner, or with either end, and put cabinets up one after the other, in sequence, checking to make sure you are putting the right one in the right place. Then put them up along the other wall, starting from the wall where you've already installed.

The screws should go through the "hanging strips" you will see at the top inside of the cabinets. The cabinets also should be screwed together through the front frames, so each run of cabinets becomes a single unit.

If yours is an L-shaped kitchen, it is best to start with the inside corner unit and screw the adjacent cabinet to it on either side, then put these three up as a single unit.

Needless to say, as each cabinet goes up you should check with a level to make sure it is straight and level, applying shims in any low spots in the wall. If you can't level it up properly, take it down and prepare the wall better. Otherwise it will only get worse. Whenever your cabinet doors are racked, it is because the wall was not prepared properly.

Now start with the corner base cabinet, attach to it the cabinet that goes on either side, and move it into position. Make sure it is true, then proceed in sequence to the end of the run. Go back to the corner already installed and proceed in sequence on the other leg.

Countertops

Now measure again for countertop size, cut your blank to fit, and lay it on the base cabinets to make sure. If it is to fit between two walls, remember that a 100-inch top absolutely will not fit in a 100-inch space between two walls. Allow 1/4 to 3/4 inch for fitting it in.

If your countertop must turn corners for an L or U kitchen, the right way is to mortise the two joining ends 45

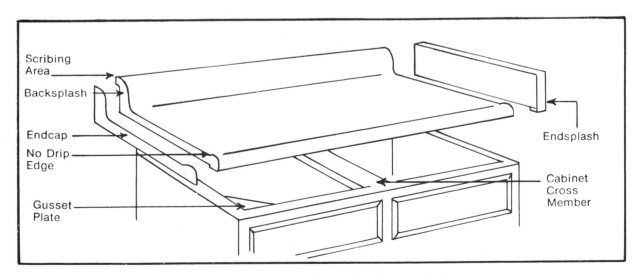

Components of a plastic laminate countertop (art courtesy of SUBA Manufacturing, Inc.).

degrees. You then will have to prepare the underside for special H-bolts which are made to hold this mortise joint together. Ask your countertop supplier for them.

When cabinets are in place, your countertop will have to be installed. Here are the basic procedures you will follow in installing your countertops. Be sure all electrical power and water supply in the working area have been turned off. Remove sink and range surface units if necessary. Use caution with any power tool, and protect your eyes.

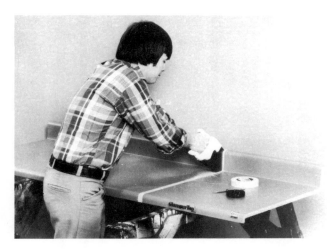

GlamourTop is the name of one of the few countertop "blanks" available over much of the U.S. They have clinics to show you how to install top and where they give you these printed instructions. In photo, note how masking tape is used to prevent chipping of plastic when sawing to size.

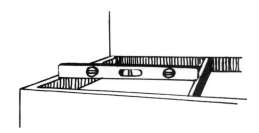

Be sure your countertop frame is level. Use a carpenter's level to determine that the cabinets are level both lengthwise and from front to back.

If cabinets are not level, use small wood shims to level the top frame when installing the countertop. It is important that

the countertop front edge hanging over the cabinets does not interfere with undercounter appliances or breadboards. If sufficient clearance is not provided, use small wood shim blocks to raise the height of the entire top, making sure these blocks are used around sink and range areas as well.

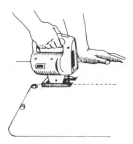

Instructions often come with the sink; you must check the size of the cutout before you begin cutting. Use the template supplied by the sink or appliance maker to mark the top side (or reverse side if using a power saw), making sure the template is square with the countertop front. A hole is first drilled within the marked cutout and then a saw is used to follow the template marking.

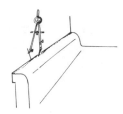

If your new counter will fit flush against the wall, place the counter in position on top of the floor cabinet and push against the countertop, forcing the backsplash flush against the wall. Use scribing kit or sharp pencil to scribe a line directly on top of the backsplash. If this line is irregular, it will be necessary to sand or file the backside of the backsplash — working toward the marked line — wherever necessary to guarantee a flush wall fit.

There are two ways to attach the counter: (1) use panel mastic; run a ribbon of panel mastic the full length of the floor cabinet top front and back. Position the top carefully on the glued area and set the counter down in place. (2) Use wood screws to go from the floor cabinet up into the counter wherever possible. If your floor cabinet has triangular-shaped pieces in the corners, this would be the best place to use screws. Now caulk along the crevice between the wall and the edge of the countertop backsplash to waterproof the area.

A clamp-type sink rim is normally used to install your sink, and complete instructions should come with the sink rim. To waterproof around the sink and range, use a good thick ribbon of caulking compound or plumbers putty where the sink-and-range rim fits on the counter. (Be sure to use the caulking or putty heavily to seal these areas — excess can be wiped off.)

Remove any excess glue, caulking, and putty.

Dishwasher

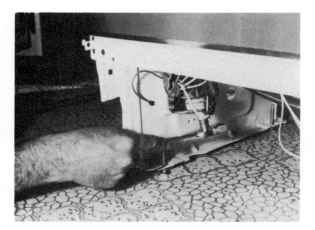

INSTALLING DISHWASHER

Adding a dishwasher unit to your kitchen is now within the ability of many home handymen. Manufacturers have designed units for this purpose and supply them with easy-to-follow instructions.

General Electric's do-it-yourself replacement kit contains all the parts needed for a typical installation such as rubber drain hose and clamps, copper water line, brass elbows and unions, and electrical connectors. An electrical test light is also provided in the kit to determine that power has been shut-off before you begin.

Installation tools required normally include a screwdriver, wire cutter, tube cutter and crescent wrench. No soldering is necessary.

Detailed instructions, diagrams and illustrations on the backside of the kit will take you through the 17 steps of removal

If you decide to put your dishwasher in now, rather than later, there are kits available that enable you to install it yourself.

First, of course, you must make sure that the appropriate provisions have been made for water and power needs. See accompanying photos for installation directions.

and replacement. (Many of these steps relate to safety and installation preparation, and are applicable even though you will not be replacing an old unit).

Steps 1-7 cover removal of the old dishwasher, starting with the water and electricity shut-off. The electric test light is used to be sure the correct circuit breaker has been thrown.

Steps 8-11 and the accompanying eight illustrations show how to alter the existing electric supply, hot water inlet plumbing, and drain connections. The remaining 6 steps outline dishwasher installation and final connection. All the dishwasher inlet and drain connections are made with quick and easy compression fittings and clamps from the kit.

The dishwasher is then leveled and fastened to the countertop's underside. After electrical connections are made, the replacement is finished. The unit is started and check is made for leaks after one completed cycle.

Lighting

Now, how are you going to light your kitchen? Kitchens generally are the most poorly-lit rooms in the house, mainly because the builder wires for one ceiling fixture only. A properly lit kitchen should have this one ceiling fixture for general illumination, and it should be on a dimmer switch so you can make it bright or dim.

Fluorescents

But there also should be what designers call "task" lighting that puts brighter light on your work areas. You can do this in many ways, such as with track lighting or recessed spots in the ceiling, but a highly-satisfactory and relatively easy way is to use fluorescent tubes under the wall cabinets.

Hopefully, you planned for these in your designing stage. Fluorescent tubes put out a lot of light with only a little power and are, in fact, about 250 percent more efficient than incandescence. So you can wire them from your wall outlets, roughing them to the exact spots in the wall where you will want to bring the wiring through the backs of the cabinets, down through the cabinet bottoms to the lights.

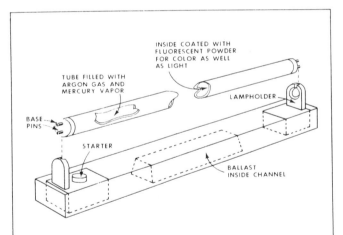

The fluorescent phosphor coating on the inside of the tube is activated by electric energy passing through the tube; light is given off. The starter in standard starter-type fixtures permits preheating of the electrodes in the ends of the tube to make it easier to start. The ballast limits the current to keep the tube functioning properly. The channel holds ballast and wiring and spaces the lampholders.

(Dept. of Agriculture).

You can find fluorescent fixtures made especially for this under-cabinet application. You will want to mount them at the bottom front of the wall cabinet — not back by the wall — and figure you'll want one 20-watt tube for each three feet of counter space. A 30-watt tube will be good for four feet, and a 40-watt tube for up to five feet. Don't be misled by these low wattages. This gives a lot of light.

Some F-I-Yers even make their own kitchen cabinets, as in this kitchen faced with Weldwood Shenandoah paneling which has natural adze marks. Here a fluorescent tube was recessed into the wall cabinet beside the window, and an island was made to hold the cooktop and provide eating space.

Try to think of interesting features for your kitchen such as this wine rack, or the condiment shelf under the wall cabinets. Wall cabinets are 12 in. deep. Shelf beneath comes out only 3 in. from wall, so it doesn't bump heads. These cabinets are faced with WilsonArt beech grain plastic laminate, and a copper metallic laminate was used between backsplash and wall cabinets. The metallic is also a WilsonArt laminate.

Large kitchen has Overton cabinets, which come unfinished, and in this case were painted sky-blue. Floor is ceramic tile, 3-in. hex pattern, in what Mid-State Tile Co. calls Blue Heron.

A small kitchen (other side of pass-through) gets added class with ceramic tile snack surface at pass-through. Tile is also on floor, a 4x5-in. hex called "Veil" by Cambridge Tile.

Make sure the overhang of the cabinet face frame hides the light from direct vision. You may have to add a shield on the bottom of the cabinet for this protection, although the fixture itself may have such a shield. If you do add such a shield it should go only low enough to hide the tube from direct vision, probably an inch or two. Paint it flat white on the light side. On the side that faces you, finish it to go with the cabinets, or use a decorative Contact paper, or a strip of plastic laminate to match the countertop.

Remember, these tubes have different colors. Most tend to have a cool, bluish cast. The "Deluxe warm white" is a little warmer in color. I use Duratest "grow" lights in my fluorescent fixtures, not for plants but because the colors are more pleasing.

For much, much more on kitchen design, lighting, color, eating facilities and other things to do in your kitchen, look for the *Book of Successful Kitchens* wherever you bought this book.

Make Your Own Cabinets

If you want to make your own kitchen cabinets, this is an example of how just one factory makes them. This is good construction. Many are worse. Some are better. But it is a guide.

Vertical members of the framework are called stiles. Horizontal members are called rails. The front rails and stiles make up the face frame, or front frame. Following is a key to the parts.

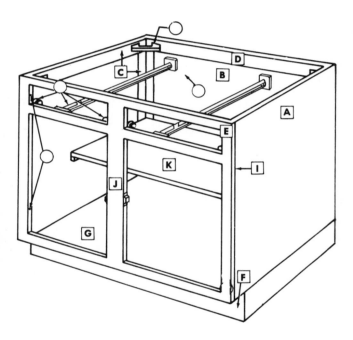

Base Cabinet

A Side panels, 1/4-inch 5-ply birch

B Back, 1/8-inch hardboard

C Sub rails and stiles (those not part of face frame), 3/4 x 5/8-inch birch

D 3/4 x 1-1/4-inch mounting rail (screwed to wall when installed)

E 3/4 x 1-1/2-inch solid birch finished frame assembly

F 3/4 x 4-inch kick rail

G 1/4-inch 5-ply cabinet bottom

H 3/16-inch scribe on finished end stiles

I 3-inch center stile on all double-door cabinets

J   12-inch-deep birch veneered fixed shelf

K   All joints glued and stapled

Note some of the numbered features: 4 — three-point drawer suspension; 5 — a block for adjusting drawer slide; 8 — predrilled mounting holes for screwing this cabinet to the next one; 9 — metal corner brace.

Wall Cabinet

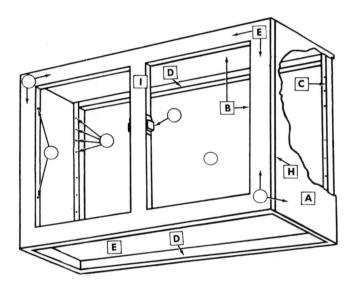

A   Side panels, 1/4-inch 5-ply birch

B   1/8-inch birch top and back

C   3/4 x 5/8-inch birch subrails and stiles

D   3/4 x 1-1/4-inch mounting rails (for screwing to wall)

E   3/4 x 1-1/2-inch solid birch finished frame assembly

F   1/4-inch 5-ply birch cabinet bottom

G   9/16 x 12-inch-deep birch-veneered adjustable shelves (not shown, but note adjustable shelf holes, no. 8)

H   3/16-inch scribe on finished end stiles

I   3-inch center stile on double-door cabinets

J   All joints glued and stapled

11. The Bathroom: Go in style

Like the kitchen, the bathroom is a room that resists change once you are through with it. It consists of a small room with three permanent fixtures, and most often you will choose fixtures in a particular color. Then you will choose a ceramic tile to match the fixtures, perhaps for floor and wainscot, perhaps for the area that surrounds the tub or shower. So you end up with a bathroom that will be, for all its life, predominantly blue, or gold, or maybe white.

So think about those fixture colors before you make your selection. Your unfinished bathroom normally will come with the fixtures installed, and whatever color you choose probably will make you happy. But remember, happy or not, you will be stuck with them for a long time, and white gives more flexibility for later changes. Most of us prefer color and are willing to be stuck with the color we choose.

Functional Design

Your bathroom probably will be roughed-in electrically for one ceiling fixture, or possibly only for an electrical medicine cabinet. Stop right there!

Design your bathroom first, just as you did your kitchen. It won't be nearly as much work as the kitchen, but it requires the fundamental element your kitchen required — space planning. So don't start to work on the walls until you have planned it, because you probably will want more wiring.

All Americans should rise in protest against the drab bathroom. This is a room in which we spend a lot of our time. It is a place to be creative. But it also is a very functional room. There are several functions that must be done there, and there are several other functions that it is desirable to do there. So, small though the room is, it can be a design triumph.

Storage

As thought-starters, let me lay a few ideas on you.

How many people will use the bathroom? It has a bearing not only on the towel bars or rings you will need, but on towel storage. Bars and rings can be added, but for storage you have to plan ahead. It also has a bearing on storage for toothpaste and hair dressing and mascara and the many other things that fill up the medicine cabinet so quickly.

How old are the people? Is there a toddler? Perhaps you need a built-in stepstool at the lavatory that he can pull out to get up there where the action is. Or, better yet, perhaps you will want to drop the counter six inches at the other end to give the youngster his or her own place, with a separate lavatory and a special medicine cabinet at a lower level. Then the adult medicine cabinet can be up, out of reach, where little hands can't get at harmful medicines.

But maybe the counter is 21 inches deep, a popular depth, and the youngster can't reach the wall, and besides, the toilet is there. So perhaps you want to curve the counter in toward the wall to a 15-inch depth, with a smaller lav, and create room around the toilet.

Now, you have a 21-inch-deep vanity at the adult lav, but then the counter drops and cuts in, and you want to utilize that storage space all the way. But they don't make a vanity in the size you want.

Alternatives

Check on kitchen wall cabinets that you can use as vanity cabinets. They come to match your vanity; they are 12 inches deep. Your adult vanity is usually 29 inches high (it varies); subtract the six inches you dropped the counter and you have 23 inches left. You can get wall cabinets 21 inches high and build a kick space under them to the height you need simply by setting them on a 2x3 or 2x4 frame. Since these are really kitchen wall cabinets they won't have drawers, but they will have adjustable shelves.

A more expensive alternative is to look for several brands of foreign cabinets now available in the U.S. Allibert specializes in bathroom cabinetry, especially in the shallower depths we've been talking about. Others are Allmilmo, Tielsa, Poggenpohl and Salvarani; you'll probably find them in the showrooms of the top kitchen dealers in your area. These dealers also will have custom U.S. lines they can adapt to your needs.

The important thing is to think storage in the bathroom. You'll need it, and it seldom is planned in.

Fixtures and Materials

First, the builder probably has provided the fixtures, and your choices are only of colors. But if he hasn't provided them, there are options open to you.

Your tub might be of cast iron, enameled steel, or the newest materials, glass fiber or cultured marble. You're already familiar with iron and steel, so we'll look at these other possibilities.

Reinforced glass fiber (usually known by the trade name "Fiberglas") can include a tub or shower stall with three walls all molded in one piece. Its big advantage is that you don't have to do anything else to the walls; they are finished when they arrive. Some of these molded jobs have seats, soap dishes and other recesses molded right in for great convenience. Some come in four pieces — tub and three walls which you must glue together with something like a latex caulk that comes with them. Installation is easy and they are very durable, but some brands are made more cheaply than others so stand in the tub or shower to check the strength and weight.

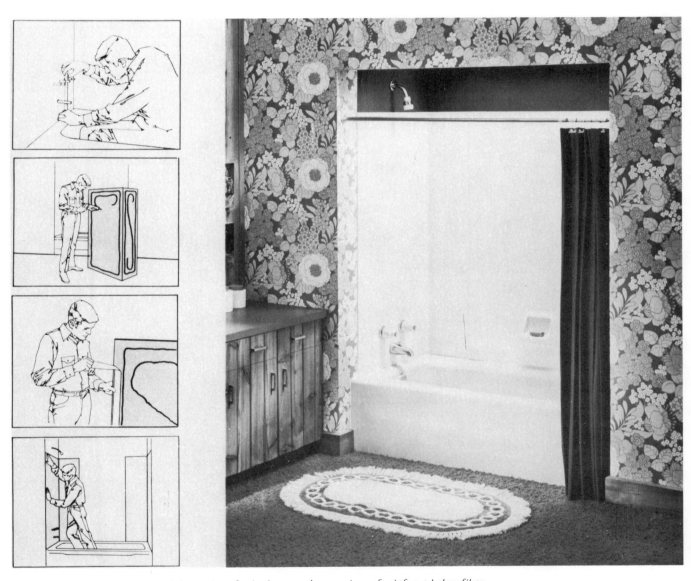

New Materials have opened the options for bathrooms. In one piece of reinforced glass fiber you can get a tub with the three walls of the tub surround and even a canopy cover. Or you can use easy fiber kits, such as this from Marlite, to form conventional tub surround. This consists of three adjustable panels for an area up to 62 in. wide and 58 in. high. Two pieces are the ends, which also turn the corners, and the third panel covers the gap between. Adhesive for installation comes with the kit.

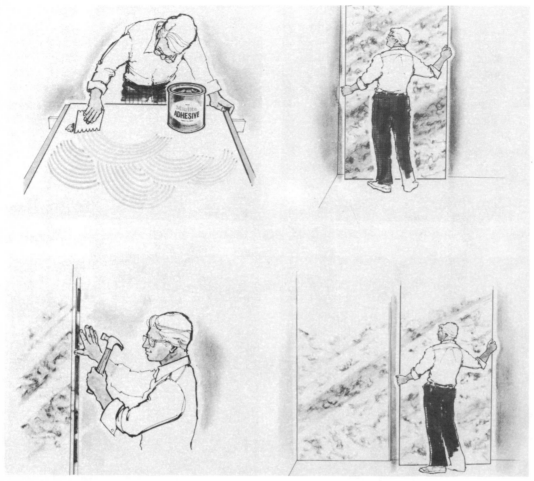

Some hardboard paneling is suitable for bathroom application, such as this Marlite. It goes up with adhesive, with molding nailed to form joints.

Cultured marble is much heavier than glass fiber. It is basically a polyester plastic that comes in colors, grained to resemble marble, and covered with a gelcoat that gives it a shine. These are spectacular and beautiful and come in many sizes and shapes. One model is heart-shaped, big enough for two, with the suggestive name of "Luv-Tub." For a cultured marble tub you can get matching wall panels in the same material, which go up with a panel adhesive.

Tubs usually are 17 inches to 18-1/2 inches high, although corner tubs usually are 14 to 16 inches high.

Standard length is 60 inches, but they range from 4 to 6 feet, except for the oversized models.

Toilets

Water closets, or toilets, are vitreous china because this is the only material that is impervious to the chemical action of body waste. But the tank that holds the reservoir of water might be of glass fiber, or other material.

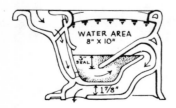

The Washdown

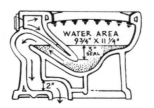

Reverse Trap

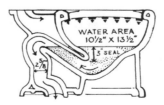

Siphon Jet

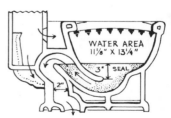

Siphon Low-Profile

120

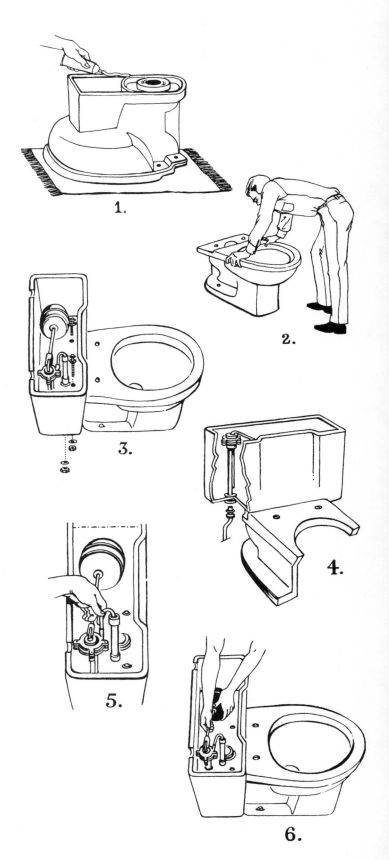

There are four types of toilets. The least expensive, least efficient and noisiest is the "washdown." It is flushed with a simple wash-out action through a trapway at the bottom of the bowl.

A step up is the "reverse trap" toilet. Flushing creates a siphon action in the trapway, assisted by a water jet at the inlet to the trapway. It is only slightly less noisy than a washdown, but much more efficient.

Another step up is the "siphon jet," which is an improvement mechanically over the reverse trap. It has a larger water surface, a larger trapway, is quieter — and more expensive.

The fourth type is the "siphon action," a name most manufacturers give to the flushing action of a low-profile, one-piece toilet and tank. They have an almost-silent flushing action, almost no dry surface in the bowl, and are considered most attractive as well as being the most expensive.

Notice that three of these might be called "siphon action" by a salesman. So look at the drawings and know the product before you pay the price.

Installation of a toilet tank and bowl begins with a thoroughly clean floor surface where the bowl is to be placed.

Place the fixture upside down on a protective, soft material to prevent scratching (1) and apply a warmed wax ring to the circular recess in the base of the bowl. This is where the fixture will be connected to the waste line plumbed through the floor. Apply a setting compound to the outer rim of the bowl to assure a continuous seal to the floor.

Carefully set the bowl atop a metal flange attached to the floor. The toilet bolts fit through holes in the base of the fixture (2), ready to receive washers and nuts, which should be secured snugly. Do not force-tighten them.

Following placement of large donut-shaped washers on the threaded tank outlet, place the tank on the ledge (3) of the bowl, and align for placement of bolts downward through the bolt holes of the two parts. Again the bolts should be tightened carefully, alternating from side to side to prevent breaking the tank or bowl.

Then connect the cold water line to the tank with a straight or angle stop (4), and insert the ballcock into the tank and secure. This later unit (5) varies in style; appropriate instructions are detailed on package.

Turn water on by opening the angle or straight stop located beneath the tank. The tank should fill to the "water line" indicated inside the tank. If not, the brass rod supporting the float ball (6) should be bent until the tank stops filling at the water line.

Sinks

Bathroom sinks are usually called "lavs," and might come in vitreous china, porcelain or cast iron, porcelain on pressed steel, carved marble or cultured marble, or glass fiber which might have either a polyester or acrylic surface.

1.

2.

3.

4.

5.

6.

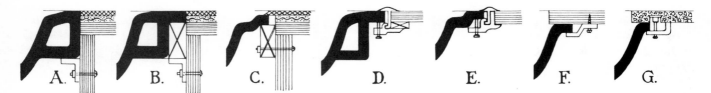

You can recess a lavatory by various means, depending upon the type of countertop selected. Diagrams A, B, and C show lavatory bowls joined with ceramic tile countertops; D, E, and F are set in decorative plastic laminate; G is set in marble.

Some lavs are wall-hung. Recently the old-fashioned pedestal sink has come back into fashion, and it is used as a fashion item. Most practical is to mount the sink of your choice in a countertop with one or more vanity cabinets underneath.

Marble, vitreous china and cast iron are the high-class materials for lavs, mounted in countertops of high-pressure plastic laminate or cast marble. The laminate, bonded to particleboard or plywood, is versatile and can be fabricated to order, with angles or flare-outs or cut-outs. But cast marble has increased in popularity in recent years, partially because of its marble-like appearance and partially because it can be bought with an integral bowl. That means you don't have to buy a separate bowl and install it.

A unique material with unique properties deserves special mention here. It is DuPont's Corian, a cultured marble that is different in that it is workable with ordinary woodworking tools. This means you can saw it, drill it, sculpt it or whatever, to fit your needs. It comes with integral bowl or without, and it is homogeneous all the way through. That means that if it ever should get a stain you can clean it with a fine sandpaper, just as you can repair nicks or scratches. It's not cheap, but it's worth the price.

In the southwest and west, ceramic tile is popular as a bathroom (or kitchen) countertop material. New manufacturing methods have made it much easier to install, but it does require grouting and the grouting always is subject to stain. But it's an attractive material, although expensive.

A. Do not lay the top where it may be stepped on, or where grit or nails may gouge it.

B. Do not peel off the protective paper—except as instructed for applying mastic and installing faucets—until <u>all</u> construction work in the room has been completed.

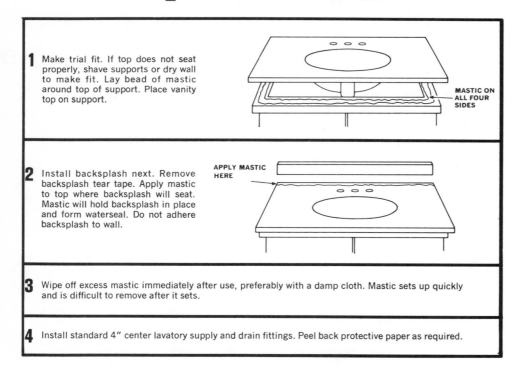

1 Make trial fit. If top does not seat properly, shave supports or dry wall to make fit. Lay bead of mastic around top of support. Place vanity top on support.

MASTIC ON ALL FOUR SIDES

2 Install backsplash next. Remove backsplash tear tape. Apply mastic to top where backsplash will seat. Mastic will hold backsplash in place and form waterseal. Do not adhere backsplash to wall.

APPLY MASTIC HERE

3 Wipe off excess mastic immediately after use, preferably with a damp cloth. Mastic sets up quickly and is difficult to remove after it sets.

4 Install standard 4" center lavatory supply and drain fittings. Peel back protective paper as required.

You can get a Corian vanity top with sink molded in to fit a standard vanity or for a whole wall. And the manufacturer provides instruction sheets, even books, to help you do it right.

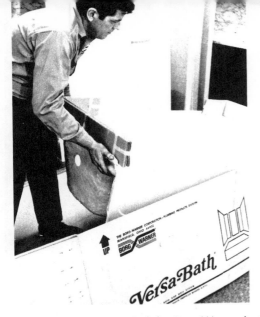

The four-piece Versa Bath by Borg-Warner includes tub and three wall panels in a single carton.

The bath unit and wall panels are secured directly to the wall studs with ordinary wood screws and patented fasteners.

The L-shaped end panels are positioned after the center panel is in place, and the outside edge again fastened with screws.

The four-piece fiberglass Versa Bath by Borg-Warner can be used for remodeling or for new construction. Installation is said to require only 90 minutes following preparation of the five-foot bath alcove, stripping of floors and walls, positioning of water and drain pipes, and installation of key studs. The Versa Bath can be supplied for right or left-hand drain, and fully assembled is 74-1/2 inches high, 60 inches long and 31-1/2 inches front-to-back. Shower doors may be attached directly to the tub panels.

The center wall panel is put in place following the leveling and securing of the bath unit.

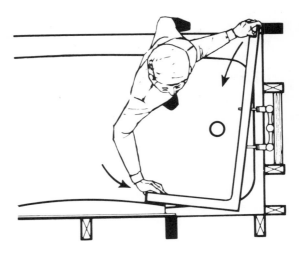

Overhead view shows the positioning of the end panel, which has been drilled to accept plumbing supply.

This glazed ceramic tile bathtub surround takes little time to install. The wainscot-height, 40-sq.-ft. package includes eight pregrouted sheets of tile, with trim attached, and two internal cover corner strips which allow for a 5/8-in. variation in size of the tub recess. Sheets can be installed over properly sealed gypsum wallboard, concrete masonry, plywood, or gypsum plaster. Silicone rubber used in the factory grouting is also used for perimeter grouting and sealing during installation. The only cutting required is for pipe holes and tub "legs." (System 310 by American Olean Tile Co.)

One-piece shower floor units can be installed faster and for lower cost than the custom lead pans often used in the construction of ceramic tile showers. (American-Standard)

The three walls around a tub or shower are called a "surround," and they might be covered with ceramic tile, Corian, cultured marble, vinyl-surfaced panels or high-pressure plastic laminate. Formica developed a surround kit, with corner moldings, that it called the "202 system," now made and marketed by an unrelated Cincinnati company called Formco. Other local fabricators have devised systems for surrounds using other laminate brands. The value is that the range of colors and patterns is almost limitless, and it is a durable, easy-upkeep material for this very moist room.

You will have to select the fittings for your lav and tub. Fittings are the lav faucets and the tub and shower valves. They come in chrome, brass, satin chrome or satin brass, antique English, antique bronze, pewter, gold, various plating, and the handles might be crystal, Lucite, any of the metals named, semi-precious metals, and "design" handles might be shaped like dolphins, rosebuds or have other special shapes.

Chrome has been the standard. If you select any of the other more delicate finishes, they will call for extra care in cleaning. With such special finishes, always read the directions on care and maintenance so you'll be aware of any problems before you buy.

In the shower or tub there are various types of pulsating showerheads. One of the best, by Moen, has a fingertip control for switching from straight shower to massage action, and another for switching to an attached hand-held unit. This is excellent versatility.

Another water appliance to consider is the whirlpool for the tub. You can get a tub with whirlpool jets built in, or you can add the appliance that hangs on the side of the tub. Built-in is better, but the side-mount is postponable if you don't want to spend the money now.

Fittings

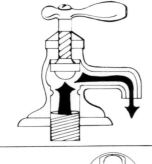

Standard Compression Valve: As illustrated on this page, two-handle faucet sets operate with threaded stems controlled by the handles. The stems screw out to open the supply port and screw in to seal the supply ports. Known as a compression valve, this type faucet has been around for nearly a hundred years.

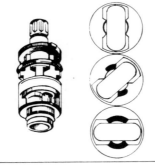

Disc-To-Disc Type: A newer, two-handle type of faucet uses disc-to-disc contact and has no threads. The lower disc is movable, controlled by a standard handle, and the other disc has ports that are exposed as the cover disc is turned. The more you turn the handle, the more the port is opened and the greater the flow of water. Full-off to full-on is accomplished by only a quarter-turn of the handle. This type faucet has no threads, washers, or packing and the o-ring is not exposed to friction or wear.

Ball-and-Socket Units: Single-handle-control faucets, which have grown greatly in popularity over the past decade, include a ball-and-socket type that operates something like an automobile stick-shift. The lever is moved up and down to control volume and left or right to control temperature. As the lever is moved, the holes in the ball line up with those in the socket.

Cartridge Type: Another type of single-lever faucet works with a cam that is pulled out to control water flow, and turned right or left for temperature control. The tapered shape of the cam controls the flow of the water by direct sealing of the ports. The interchangeable cartridge has no metal-to-metal friction and is self-adjusting and self-lubricating. If the faucet requires maintenance, the entire cartridge is replaced.

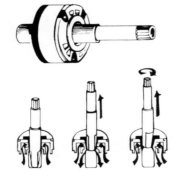

Tapered Cam Mechanism: Still another of the newest types on the market is the single-handle unit with a cam that is pulled out to control water flow. The tapered shape controls water volume by opening and sealing ports. Here again, turning the handle left or right controls temperature. This kind of faucet is easy to operate, is permanently lubricated and its single moving part is completely isolated from water to provide years of maintenance-free usage.

When you purchase a faucet, ask the seller for a written warranty. Quality faucets, like other appliances, have written warranties to back them up.

Ventilation and Heat

Your houseplan may have provided for ventilation and heat in the bathroom. Check it and see. If not, you will want to add both before the room is finished off.

Ventilation not only removes odor, it also removes the excess moisture that comes with a hot shower. Without forced ventilation, a hot shower will cloud every mirror in the room and put dripping water on the walls.

In such a case, the moisture input is tremendous. It takes a powerful fan to remove it, and also a lot of air leakage into the bathroom to permit the exchange of air. Ventilating fans are rated by the Home Ventilating Institute for air movement, and you'll find the rating on the unit. This rating often is insufficient if you like real hot showers, and I recommend a more powerful unit.

You can buy a combination ventilating-heating unit for the ceiling or wall, or one that includes light. If you do you will need to wire for three switches at the door, one for the fan, one for heat and one for light.

There are two kinds of heat to consider in this fixture. In one type, the unit has electric resistance heat that is fan-forced into the bathroom. This is good, but it takes a little time to warm the room and electrical resistance heat is very expensive. The alternative is a radiant heat bulb. It doesn't warm the room, but it warms any object in the path of the radiant energy, and does it instantly. This is commonly used in motels.

Another possible heat source is made by Intertherm. It is made to fit under a cabinet, in the kickspace, and provides hot water heat in a sealed unit, electrically heated, with fan and thermostat. There are three 1000-watt models, each with 2400 btu output, and they are 22 inches long, 14 inches deep and 3-1/2 inches high. They can be wired or can plug into a wall outlet; if you plan on this put a wall outlet out of sight near the floor.

If you are the steambath type, it is a simple thing to buy a small steam generator for the tub or shower stall. You'll have to plumb it into the hot water line and bring it out even with the faucets, and wire it for the small amount of heat to make the steam. And you'll have to seal in the tub or shower enclosure a little more tightly to hold the steam in.

Ordinary tub enclosure can be converted to steam room with Thermasol steam generator. And it looks about the same. Here a full sliding vapor/shatter-proof enclosure replaces more customary shower curtain (A) and you simply have to plumb in the pipe and steam control. Generator can go in vanity base (B) or in wasted area over tub enclosure (C) or even in remote location such as a closet (D).

Ⓑ

Ⓓ

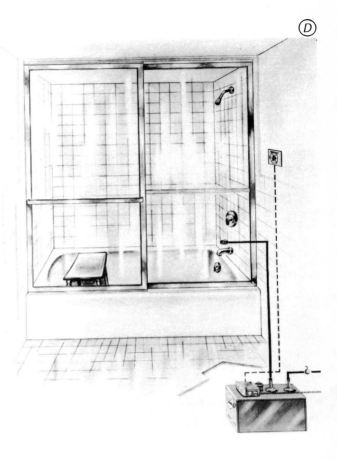

Ⓒ

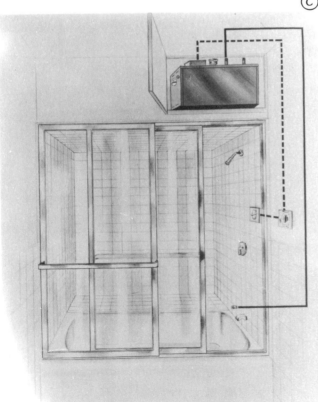

Flooring

Your flooring choices are ceramic tile, resilient flooring and carpet. The latter is not the most practical, but it is increasingly popular. Other lesser-used choices are terrazzo, marble and applied seamless flooring (see earlier chapter on floors).

No-wax resilient sheet goods would be the most practical, and they offer very wide variety of colors and patterns. It will be more comfortable if cushioned. Ceramic tile is very widely used and makes an excellent floor for the bathroom. You can add a washable throw rug for warmth. Bathroom carpeting offers two choices. One is the washable shag, quite popular, which can be installed with a 2-sided tape around the perimeter and can be lifted easily for washing. The other is kitchen carpeting, which has an impermeable membrane between the nap and the sponge rubber backing. This goes down permanently with a 2-sided tape around the perimeter, although the instructions usually call for an overall adhesive. You can wash or scrub it in place. Water won't go through it.

Seamless flooring, often known as "poured" flooring, is an extremely durable plastic into which you scatter chips of marble or other decorative materials. When it dries it is there forever. It is used more for commercial floors, and was used in the corridors of the Astrodome in Houston. It still looks like new. You can do it yourself from instructions on the packages.

The easiest solution for covering what remains of the walls is paint. It is easy to apply and easy to change. You can add decorator touches on one wall or parts of walls with sheet vinyl-coated fabrics. But it also is possible to cover the walls with Corian or other cultured marble, or panels of wood or plastic laminate. You also can use ceramic tile, or glass fiber panels. Ceramic tile now is available in pregrouted sheets, making it easier to apply (see earlier chapters).

Floor Plans

Want to improve your bathroom in easy ways that don't cost a fortune? Here are some suggestions from Eljer Plumbingware, showing the simple bath as it might be delivered by a builder, and a suggested change to improve it. The improvements range from addition of vanity cabinets and medicine cabinets to relocation of fixtures for more space. Remember, always look for places where you can add cabinets.

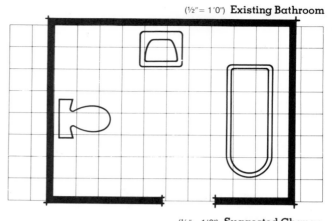

(½" = 1'0") **Existing Bathroom**

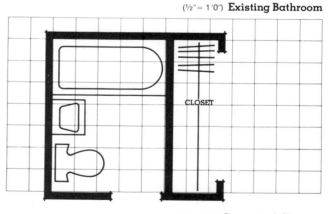

(½" = 1'0") **Suggested Change**

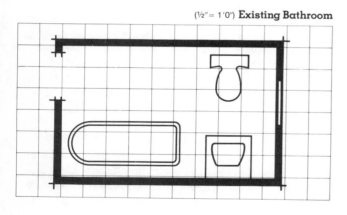

(½" = 1'0") **Existing Bathroom**

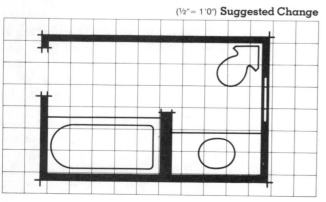

(½" = 1'0") **Suggested Change**

(½" = 1'0") **Existing Bathroom**

CLOSET

(½" = 1'0") **Suggested Change**

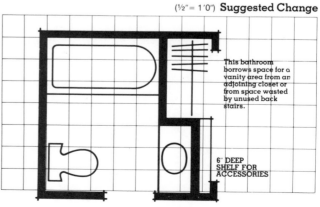

This bathroom borrows space for a vanity area from an adjoining closet or from space wasted by unused back stairs.

6" DEEP SHELF FOR ACCESSORIES

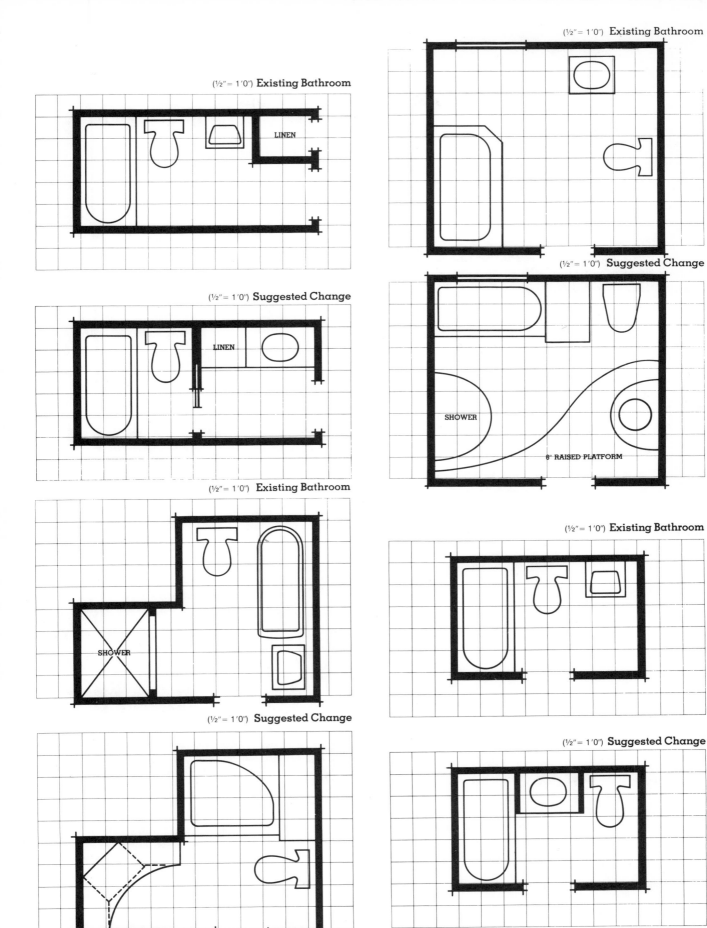

(½″ = 1′0″) **Existing Bathroom**

LINEN

(½″ = 1′0″) **Suggested Change**

LINEN

(½″ = 1′0″) **Existing Bathroom**

SHOWER

(½″ = 1′0″) **Suggested Change**

(½″ = 1′0″) **Existing Bathroom**

(½″ = 1′0″) **Suggested Change**

SHOWER

6″ RAISED PLATFORM

(½″ = 1′0″) **Existing Bathroom**

(½″ = 1′0″) **Suggested Change**

129

12. Garages: Conversions and room additions

There are some who contend that if God had wanted houses to have garages, He wouldn't have put driveways in front of them where you can put your car after you fill the garage up with junk.

A garage is a good place to put a car overnight, especially for those who live in the north. But it also represents a lot of usable living space, if converted; today many, many homeowners are opting for just that.

A garage that's remote from the house may have to be built up structurally, and its use would be more limited. But it could be converted into a playroom for children or a party room for adults.

Structural Work, Wiring

But the garage connected to the house and under the same roof is ideal for any purpose. Its structure probably will be the same as house structure, and the problems would be simply to build up the floor, finish the interior, and fill in the doorway.

Floors

There are two reasons for building up the floor. First, garage floors are usually at ground level and water can come in during rainy periods. Second, a concrete floor would be subject to the same moisture condensation-problems as a basement floor, so it would need a flooring structure for carpeting, hardwood flooring, or other floor covering.

If the floor isn't raised, you can solve the water problem by making sure the outside ground slopes away from the garage on all sides, and that the eaves do not dump rain water right at the foundation. A good precaution would be to cut a trench all around, and fill the trench with stone to take water away.

The floor can be raised simply by installing floor joists across the enclosed area, from the base plate on one side to the base plate on the other, then adding a subfloor (see Chapter 7). This probably would leave a step or two down from the level of the house floor to the new garage floor, and you would have to build the step.

But the best way would be to raise the garage floor so it would be even with the house floor. This would

incorporate your new space more subtly into the house, and also would provide a crawl space beneath for later additions of wiring or plumbing. This can be done easily by adding 2x4s to raise the base plate on either side, so the addition of 2x6 joists plus 1/2-inch plywood subfloor, plus floor covering will come out even with the house floor.

If, however, you will lay your new joists on the existing base plates, prepare for eventualities by bringing in new wiring. Drill holes in the joists to bring a circuit to the far wall before you fill in the floor.

Insulation

You already know about insulation. Don't forget it here. Lay in a vapor barrier and insulation between the new joists, and use a vapor barrier with the insulation between the wall studs. And insulate along the roof.

1. Here's a representative garage, perhaps similar to yours. You may keep the car outside much of the time, anyway, and would like to convert it to living space. This series suggests one way (Photos by the American Plywood Assn.).

2. *Draw your plan first. Check window sizes that are available, etc. Then cut hole in side wall.*

5. *To finish off the front outside, you extend roof rafters and floor joists, use vertical 2x4 studs for pattern and horizontal slats to protect from afternoon sun.*

3. *You'll want to take that garage door off and frame the opening. You'll extend the floor framing out in the new opening you cut in the side.*

6. *Here's what it looks like from your front door — neat, trim, with a lot of glass for light.*

4. *Here's a look at the framing of the new hole you cut in the side, looking from garage doorway. Note you have added insulation and put up a wallboard ceiling. You won't have to tape and spackle it because your plan calls for a painted plywood ceiling to finish it off.*

7. *And that hole you cut in the wall? You frame it for window glass, cut a vent hole through its roof, and through the house roof for a new fireplace.*

This is a typical carport, still in its original form.

8. *Here are two views of the new room. The fireplace is in the back corner of what was the garage, between the run of built-in sofas, all constructed of plywood. Windows at right look out where garage door used to be, with slats obstructing view of car and driveway. You can get more complete details on this job by writing the American Plywood Assn.; (see address in appendix).*

Here's another that stayed the same, a garage.

This homeowner simply filled in the front, and added a door and windows on the front and side for use as another room.

Homeowners do a lot of different things to make their garages livable. To prove it, we drove through the world's first famous housing development, Levittown PA, built 25 years ago. The photos here show what we found.

Look these over before you plan your own conversion. You can guess what costs more, what costs less, but note especially how well the conversions fit the house to get some idea of what you will and won't like.

This bigger home had a 2-car garage, which added a sizable living area in character with the house.

One of simplest conversions added door at side, front window unit to match others, and shutters.

The plain vanilla conversion added only a window in front.

Here the front window unit matches the garage door opening. Again, a new door is added at the side.

This homeowner put a fireplace in his converted garage, by building a chimney on the outside.

Added door wasn't needed in this small house. The garage was simply framed, finished off, and window units added.

Here the owner kept the covering for a car, but closed in and finished off a small utility room at the back.

If you need your garage, add a room elsewhere

To build an addition on your house, frame it the same way all the rest of the house is framed. Call in a contractor to build the foundation* and then frame with 2x4 lumber. In this example by Champion International, all framing is 16 inches on center because most of the codes are written that way. This addition, however, will have 1/2-inch plywood sheathing, which will make it extremely strong so that 24 inches on center would be adequate if the building code permits.

Sheathing can be applied vertically or horizontally. Horizontal, with face grain across supports, is stronger. Nail the first panel of sheathing and check for accuracy with a level. Continuing with sheathing; note that ends of panels will come naturally at studs. Make sure they do.

This addition will take Weldwood panel siding, which can be applied direct to the studs. In the case shown here, sheathing was wanted also, adding greatly to strength and durability.

*For do-it-yourself specifics on foundations, framing and roofing, consult **Successful Homes Additions** by Joseph Schram, or **How to Build Your Own Home** by Robert Reschke.

Sheathing goes on the header also, for flat siding application. Apply roof sheathing also, before siding goes on. Use a circular saw to trim sheathing even with wall. Cover roof sheathing with paper, then apply shingles.

Window unit comes next. You will have sized this opening for the prebuilt window unit. Level it.

Outside felt paper could be eliminated because of sheathing, but it will provide extra moisture protection. Nail at 12-inch intervals. The addition is now ready for siding. Here, Champion International's Planktex is used. Along edges, nails should be at 6-inch intervals. Otherwise that should be 12 inches. Use 6d nails.

A corner board is nailed over siding for accent. Caulk thoroughly around all joints and openings.

Nail soffit in place, cut hole for louvered vent and install a louvered vent. Cut molding and nail into place. Note that regular plywood is used for soffit. The siding material could be used.

The finished siding can be left to weather naturally. But Champion recommends it be finished for protection against weather. Use a high-quality oil base or latex emulsion stain.

Manufacturers' Addresses

American Olean Tile Co., 1000 Cannon Av., Lansdale PA 19446

American Plywood Assn., 1119 A. St., Tacoma WA 98401

Armstrong Cork Co., Liberty & Charlotte, Lancaster PA 17604

Borden Chemical, 180 E. Broad St., Columbus OH 43215

Borg-Warner (BW Plumbing Products) 201 E. 5th St., Mansfield OH 44901

CertainTeed Products, Box 860, Valley Forge PA 19482

Champion Building Products, 1 Landmark Sq., Stamford CT 06921

DuPont de Nemours, Tatnall Bldg., Products Information Section, Wilmington DE 19898

Eljer Plumbingware, 3 Gateway Center, Pittsburgh PA 15222

Georgia/Pacific Corp., 900 SW Fifth Av., Portland OR 97204

H. C. Products Co., Box 68, Princeville, IL 61159

Home Ventilating Institute, 230 N. Michigan Av., Chicago IL 60601

Interwall, Interior Products Grp., 850 Third Av., New York NY 10022

Joanna Western, 2141 S. Jefferson St., Chicago IL 60616

Leigh Products, 1536 Grant St., Elkhart IN 46514

Living Walls, 120 E. 144 St., New York NY 10451

Marlite Div., Masonite, Dover OH 44622

Masonite Corp., 29 W. Wacker Dr., Chicago IL 60606

National Decorating Products Assn., 9334 Dillman Industrial Dr., St. Louis, MO 63132

National Mineral Wool Insulation Assn., 211 E. 51st St., New York N.Y. 10022

Ridge Homes, 501 Office Center Dr., Ft. Washington PA 19034

St. Charles Mfg. Co., 1611 E. Main St., St. Charles IL 60174

Skymaster Corp., 413 Virginia Dr., Orlando FL 32803

Western Wood Molding & Millwork Producers,

Index

Adhesives, types of 15
Appliances, major kitchen 103
Attic ventilation 90
    Power vent chart 91

Basement ideas 63
    Moisture elimination 62
Bathroom, design 118
    Storage 118
    Faucets 125
    Heat and ventilation .126
    Flooring 127
    Steambath 126
    Walls 38, 41, 42
Bathtubs 119
    Tub surrounds 38, 123
Bridging (between joists) 16

Cabinets, kitchen, construction 116
    Styles 109
    Types 104
Carpeting, wall-to-wall 56
    Shag installation 58
    Squares 59
Ceilings, gypsum board .46
    Painting 24, 46
    Papering 48
    Suspended 49
    Texturing 46
    Tiles 48
Closets 17
Countertops, Installing .112
    Space needed 106
    Tile 41
    Types 109

Dishwashers 103
    Installation 114
Dormers 96, 99
Doors, clearance, framing 17

Electrical circuits 95

Flooring, hardwood, installation 54
    Resilient, installation 53, 59
    Types of 53
    Underlayment 54

Garage, conversion 130

Housekeeping rooms 70
Headers, door, window .17

Insulation, attic 89
    Installing in wall 20
    Payback on investment 13
    Recommended amounts 13
    Where to insulate 12

Kitchens, basic measurements 102
    Cabinets 103
    Countertops 109
    How to design 105
    How to plan 101
    Installing 110
    Lighting 115
    Optional ways to buy 100
    Shapes 101
    Work triangle 102

Laundries 70
Lavatories, bathroom 121
Lighting, kitchen 115

Moldings, use of 24
    Coping, mitering 26

Nails, types of 14

Partitions 16

Room, adding to house 134

Screws, types of. 14
Sinks, types 103
    Bathroom lavs 121
    Installation 113

Skylights 96-98

Tile, ceramic, countertop 41
    How to install 37
    Tub surround 38, 124
Toilet installation. 121
    Types of 120
Tub surrounds, tile. .38, 41
    Corian 42
    Other surrounds. 123

Ventilating hoods, kitchen .103
Ventilation, attic 89

Wallboard, how to cut 21
    How to install 21
    Taping, spackling 22
Wallcovering 22
    How to apply 23
Wall paneling, how to install. 27
    On Masonry wall 29
    Plant type 32
Walls, insulating 20
    Painting. 24
    Storage 16, 18
    Temporary 16
Wiring tips 94

Other SUCCESSFUL Books

SUCCESSFUL SPACE SAVING AT HOME. The conquest of inner space in apartments, whether tiny or ample, and homes, inside and out. Storage and built-in possibilities for all living areas, with a special section of illustrated tips from the professional space planners. 8½" x 11"; 128 pp; over 150 B-W and color photographs and illustrations. $12.00 Cloth. $4.95 Paper.

BOOK OF SUCCESSFUL HOME PLANS. Published in cooperation with Home Planners, Inc.; designs by Richard B. Pollman. A collection of 226 outstanding home plans, plus information on standards and clearances as outlined in HUD's *Manual of Acceptable Practices.* 8½" x 11"; 192 pp; over 500 illustrations. $12.00 Cloth. $4.95 Paper.

HOW TO CUT YOUR ENERGY BILLS, Derven and Nichols. A homeowner's guide designed not for just the fix-it person, but for everyone. Instructions on how to save money and fuel in all areas—lighting, appliances, insulation, caulking, and much more. If it's on your utility bill, you'll find it here. 8½" x 11"; 136 pp; over 200 photographs and illustrations. $12.00 Cloth. $4.95 Paper.

FINDING & FIXING THE OLDER HOME, Schram. Tells how to check for tell-tale signs of damage when looking for homes and how to appraise and finance them. Points out the particular problems found in older homes, with instructions on how to remedy them. 8½" x 11"; 160 pp; over 200 photographs and illustrations. $12.00 Cloth. $4.95 Paper.

WALL COVERINGS AND DECORATION, Banov. Describes and evaluates different types of papers, fabrics, foils and vinyls, and paneling. Chapters on art selection, principles of design and color. Complete installation instructions for all materials. 8½" x 11"; 136 pp; over 150 B-W and color photographs and illustrations. $12.00 Cloth. $4.95 Paper.

BOOK OF SUCCESSFUL KITCHENS, Galvin. In-depth information on building, decorating, modernizing, and using kitchens, by the editor of *Kitchen Business* magazine. 8½" x 11"; 136 pp.; over 200 B-W and color photographs and illustrations. $12.00 Cloth. $4.95 Paper.

BOOK OF SUCCESSFUL PAINTING, Banov. Everything about painting any surface, inside or outside. Includes surface preparation paint selection and application, problems, and color in decorating. "Before dipping brush into paint, a few hours spent with this authoritative guide could head off disaster."—*Publishers Weekly.* 8½" x 11"; 114 pp; over 150 B-W and color photographs and illustrations. $12.00 Cloth. $4.95 Paper.

BOOK OF SUCCESSFUL BATHROOMS, Schram. Complete guide to remodeling or decorating a bathroom to suit individual needs and tastes. Materials are recommended that have more than one function, need no periodic refinishing, and fit into different budgets. Complete installation instructions. 8½" x 11"; 128 pp; over 200 B-W and color photographs. (Chosen by Interior Design, Woman's How-to, and Popular Science Book Clubs) $12.00 Cloth. $4.95 Paper.

TOTAL HOME PROTECTION, Miller. How to make your home burglarproof, fireproof, accidentproof, termiteproof, windproof, and lightningproof. With specific instructions and product recommendations. 8½'' x 11''; 124 pp; over 150 photographs and illustrations. (Chosen by McGraw-Hill's Architects Book Club) $12.00 Cloth. $4.95 Paper.

BOOK OF SUCCESSFUL SWIMMING POOLS, Derven and Nichols. Everything the present or would-be pool owner should know, from what kind of pool he can afford and site location, to construction, energy savings, accessories and maintenance and safety. 8½'' x 11''; over 250 B-W and color photographs and illustrations; 128 pp. $12.00 Cloth. $4.95 Paper.

HOW TO **BUILD YOUR OWN HOME,** Reschke. Construction methods and instructions for woodframe ranch, one-and-a-half story, two-story, and split level homes, with specific recommendations for materials and products. 8½'' x 11''; 336 pages; over 600 photographs, illustrations, and charts. (Main selection for McGraw-Hill's Engineers Book Club) $14.00 Cloth. $5.95 Paper.

SUCCESSFUL STUDIOS AND WORK CENTERS, Davidson. How and where to set up work centers at home for the professional or amateur—for art projects, photography, sewing, woodworking, pottery and jewelry, or home office work. The author covers equipment, floor plans, basic light/plumbing/wiring requirements, and adds interviews with artists, photographers, and other professionals telling how they handled space and work problems. 8½'' x 11''; 144 pp; over 200 photos and diagrams. $12.00 Cloth. $4.95 Paper.

SUCCESSFUL FAMILY AND RECREATIONS ROOMS, Cornell. How to best use already finished rooms or convert spaces such as garage, basement, or attic into family/recreation rooms. Along with basics like lighting, ventilation, plumbing, and traffic patterns, the author discusses ''mood setters'' (color schemes, fireplaces, bars, etc.) and finishing details (flooring, wall covering, ceilings, built-ins, etc.). A special chapter gives quick ideas for problem areas. 8½'' x 11''; 144 pp; over 250 photos and diagrams. (Featured alternate for McGraw-Hill Book Clubs.) $12.00 Cloth. $4.95 Paper.

SUCCESSFUL HOME GREENHOUSES, Scheller. Instructions, complete with diagrams, for building all types of greenhouses. Among topics covered are: site location, climate control, drainage, ventilation, use of sun, auxiliary equipment, and maintenance. Charts provide characteristics and requirements of plants and greenhouse layouts are included in appendices. ''One of the most completely detailed volumes of advice for those contemplating an investment in a greenhouse.'' *Publishers Weekly.* 8½'' x 11''; 136 pp; over 200 photos and diagrams. (Featured alternates of the Popular Science and McGraw-Hill Book Clubs). $12.00 Cloth. $4.95 Paper.

BOOK OF SUCCESSFUL FIREPLACES, 20th ed., Lytle. The expanded, updated edition of the book that has been a standard of the trade for over 50 years—over a million copies sold! Advice is given on selecting from the many types of fireplaces available, on planning and adding fireplaces, on building fires, on constructing and using barbecues. Also includes new material on wood as a fuel, woodburning stoves, and energy savings. 8½'' x 11''; 128 pp; over 250 photos and illustrations. $12.00 Cloth. $5.95 Paper.

Structures Publishing Company   Box 423   Farmington, Michigan 48024